Praise
The Marital Mystery Tour by Alan & Pauly Heller

The Marital Mystery Tour is written from a fresh, unique perspective. Alternately a novel and an instructional guide, this book provides an intimate look at both the male and female viewpoints in a marriage. As we read Marital Mystery Tour, we laughed as we recognized some of the familiar paths of miscommunication we have taken in our own marriage and we gained new understanding and respect for one another as we realized what our actions and statements look like from the "other side".

Eric and Jennifer Garcia
Co-Founders, Association of Marriage and Family Ministries (AMFM)

If you were new to a city, what would you rather have… a map shoved in your hand or a personal guide to show you the sites, safe places and areas to avoid? The answer is obvious, and the need is the same for those just starting out in marriage – or those wanting to get to a new, more positive place in their marriage. Alan and Pauly Heller can be that *"personal guide"* you need to take the next step in your marriage. I've known them for almost two decades, and seen them walk alongside couples and families in a powerful, positive, God-honoring way. Now that wisdom they've shared face-to-face with couples for years is captured here in a book that takes you on a Marital Mystery Tour – one *your* marriage needs to take today!

John Trent, Ph.D.
President, The Center for StrongFamilies and StrongFamilies.com
Author of The Blessing and The 2 Degree Difference

The Marital Mystery Tour

*Five Keys to Unlock
Marital Mysteries*

The Marital Mystery Tour

Five Keys to Unlock Marital Mysteries

Alan & Pauly Heller

ISBN: 978-0-9796620-0-3
Library of Congress Control Number: 2007928970

We dedicate this book to our parents, J. Leonard and Lisa Burger, and George and Connie Heller, whose 50-plus-year marriages demonstrated to us that it's possible to choose to remain contentedly married "'til death us do part," and to Dr. Howard Hendricks, through whose messages, both taped and live, we received the solid biblical foundation in the inerrant Word of God on which our marriage stands.

Contents

Acknowledgements

I don't think this book would even have been started without the encouragement of the Phoenix Christian Writers group and their astute leader, Vic Kelly.

To John Trent and Tim Kimmel, thank you for encouraging us to push beyond what we thought we could do.

We owe a huge spiritual debt of gratitude to the many friends who prayed for us throughout this project, especially Michael and Helen Johnston and their home fellowship group, the ladies of Grace Chapel at whose retreat Pauly repented of her sin and disobedience in dragging her feet for so long, her precious sisters from the Thursday morning Bible study at Cheryl Watkins' house, and all who have prayed for us and Walk & Talk over the years.

Special thanks to Greg and Cindy Reynolds for reading the manuscript and giving us their very helpful comments; to Elizabeth Benham, who not only read the manuscript, but also allowed us the elegant privacy of her and Robert's lovely home as our personal writing retreat.

We are immensely grateful to Lisa Koziol, who is probably capable of typing a thousand and one words per minute; she retyped and formatted the entire manuscript for us.

And to John Keeney and Eric and Jennifer Garcia, thank you for giving us this opportunity to join the AMFM family and represent this vital ministry in print.

Introduction

Alan and I have always been excited about passing along to others whatever we have learned about life and relationships. Unfortunately, in the early years of our marriage, we didn't have enough experience to pass along much. But about ten years into our marriage, we developed a notebook called "How to Have a Triple-R Weekend." We based it on wisdom we had gleaned from the leadership of Campus Crusade for Christ who encouraged staff members to get away from the pressures of ministry for personal times of refreshment. An architect from our Sunday school class illustrated it with clever drawings, and another friend created its graphic design.

Excited about our creation, we showed it to our friends Tim Kimmel and John Trent, both nationally recognized speakers and authors, in hopes that they could help us get our "baby" birthed into a bestseller. "This is nice, it would make a good companion piece to a book on marriage," Tim told us during lunch. Discouraged, but not destroyed, we licked our wounded pride and limped back to the word processor.

Not long afterward, we were asked to speak to a couples group and created a talk on five keys to unlock the mysteries of marriage. We created five C's to help the group remember the five keys: Comradeship, Commitment, Communication, Completeness, and Consecration. Alan was the clever one who declared, "We can call it 'The Marital Mystery Tour.'"

Now we had a great title for a book; all we had to do was write it. Unfortunately, I was swamped with home schooling our three children, being a soccer mom, and helping Alan lead communication workshops which were all very convenient excuses to help me procrastinate while I wrestled with my fears of failure. Over the next few years, I joined a Christian writers group and attended enough conferences to realize that even with my B.A. in English, I still had a lot to learn about writing.

Meanwhile, Alan and I kept plugging away at the book. He's great with ideas; I just make them readable and grammatically correct. Tim and John encouraged us in our efforts. John even helped us get to a Christian Booksellers Association convention in California, where we handed out book proposals to every acquisitions editor who would give us eye contact. "This is a clever title," said one. "But where in your book does the tour come in?"

Hmmm, we hadn't thought about that. So back to the computer I went, creating the characters David and Marsha—our middle names—who are invited by a mysterious stranger to tour some property they've inherited, an estate that represents their marriage. The months stretched into years as I developed back-stories and plot lines worthy of a first novel. The project was becoming far too complicated, David and Marsha argued too much to be likable, and I was losing sight of our main objective, which was to teach five keys to unlock marital mysteries.

Perhaps Alan and I needed to get a few more years of marriage experience under our belts, or maybe I needed to get over my fears and just write the book. I finally devised a structure that I thought would work. I would retain the idea of a couple receiving an inheritance through a mysterious stranger, but the couple would be more generic; a man and a woman to whom, I hope, many readers will relate. They experience identical circumstances, but perceive them through uniquely male and female perspectives. Throughout the book I introduce each chapter with the female point of view ("LADIES FIRST") then the male perspective ("AND GENTLEMEN") followed by Alan's and my own observations and teaching.

We realize that not every characteristic of these stereotypes will fit all of our readers, but we hope that enough of them will relate to enough of you so that you will see some of yourself in them and benefit from their experiences. We hope you'll find the trip enjoyable as you embark on your own *Marital Mystery Tour*.

SECTION ONE:
The Key of Comradeship

chapter one

WELCOME TO THE MARITAL MYSTERY TOUR

LADIES FIRST

Picture this: You answer a *tap-tap-tap* at the door. There stands a tall man in a tailored business suit. *What can such an elegantly dressed guy want with us*, you wonder. *He's too well dressed for a salesman.* Slightly bowing, he says, "I am Mr. Michaels and I represent . . . ." The rest of his sentence is lost in a huge clap of thunder. *That's weird*, you think, glancing up at the clear, sunny sky.

You and your husband have inherited a magnificent estate from a fabulously rich relative, Mr. Michaels explains, and he wants to take you there the following morning. "So will you please inform your husband and be ready to go tomorrow morning at 8 o'clock?"

"Sure," you say, "whatever." But closing the door, you think maybe he's duping you into one of those timeshare presentations and you should just cancel and forget about it. So you reopen the door, but Mr. Michaels has vanished. *Where did he go so quickly*, you marvel.

Bemused, you walk back to the family room, where your husband is planted in front of an endless string of TV sports shows. "Honey, the strangest thing just happened," you begin. You tell him about Mr. Michaels, the thunder, and the estate. He gives you that look that he thinks looks like he's listening, but you know he's really still watching the game. *All right*, you decide, *I guess I'll have to wait and see what happens.*

But waiting is hard and sleeping is harder. You're exhausted from a busy day, but as soon as your head hits the pillow, the little "thought mice" start running around inside your brain. *Is this guy for real? Did we really get an inheritance? Is this going to end up costing us thousands of dollars? I'll bet it's a pyramid scheme, like selling room deionizers or vitamins or aloe vera juice products,* the thought mice insist. Every half hour you're looking at the clock until you finally doze off around 3:30.

As dawn breaks, you drag yourself out of bed and into the shower. What's an appropriate outfit for touring an estate? You stand in front of your closet trying to decide whether to dress up or just throw on jeans and a T-shirt in case Mr. Michaels doesn't make an appearance. You compromise—a new pair of jeans with a light gray sweater and a bit of makeup. Promptly at 8, a *tap-tap-tap (How did I manage to hear that over the sound of the running dishwasher and the clothes dryer?)* sends you flying to the front door.

"Honey, he's here!" you yell in the general direction of the computer desk, where your husband sits paying bills. "Are you ready to go?"

"Who's here? Go where?" he mutters to the checkbook. When he looks up and sees you standing expectantly in the doorway with the immaculately attired Mr. Michaels, you realize with embarrassment that your dearly beloved hasn't shaved and he's wearing a faded polo shirt and the stained Levi's he wore the last time he painted the living room.

He jumps up out of his chair as you mumble an introduction. Mr. Michaels holds out his hand, and your husband shakes it. They walk to the front door chatting like old buddies, and you run to the kitchen to grab your purse and scurry after them out the door. That's when you see the sleek, gleaming white limousine. And what's happened to your husband? Wasn't he just dressed like a schlump? You blink at his freshly shaved face, combed hair and crisply pressed button-down shirt.

"Come on, hon, you're keeping us waiting," he says from the back seat of the limo. "Mr. Michaels is taking us on a tour of our new property." Luckily for him, you fight the urge to strangle him.

Visions of The Trump World Tower collide with skepticism as you leave the city limits. "Do you think he's for real?" you whisper to your husband. "I mean, this could still be some kind of gigantic, expensive hoax, don't you think?"

"Honey, I don't know. I'm just going to wait and see. Why don't you relax and enjoy the ride?"

Why does he always talk to me like I'm a total idiot, you in-wardly fume as you turn away from him and stare out the window. The limo rounds a bend in the road, and you approach burnished brass gates ornately inscribed with the words "Your Marriage." *This feels like a dream,* you think, and your heart pounds as you look around for hidden cameras. You're about to ask Mr. Michaels if you're on a new television reality show when he turns to you with a formal smile.

"Welcome to your Marital Mystery Tour," he begins. "All you see within these grounds belongs to the two of you. My job is to show you its buildings and describe all they may contain for you. However, their actual contents will remain a mystery until you take the keys I hand you and explore them for yourselves."

Your mouth drops open as your eyes scan the acreage stretched out before you—a pillared mansion and landscaped lawn set amid cultivated fields, a brightly painted barn and silo, manicured flower gardens, and grassy hillsides dotted with grazing cattle and horses.

"There is much more here than meets the eye," Mr. Michaels continues. "The wealth of your estate is infinite, extending far be-yond what you see from here."

"Let us begin with the main house. Ah, here is the one." He chooses a polished key from the ring attached to his vest pocket. It catches the sunlight as he extends his hand toward the two of you. "This is the key of Comradeship."

"Well, you'd better give it to me," you say. "'He loses everything." And you clip it onto a key ring attached to your purse.

AND GENTLEMEN

Okay, guys: So you're in the middle of an NBA game when your wife bursts into the TV room with some crazy story about a door-to-door salesman with one of those "You have a chance to win . . ." schemes. She insists he's not a salesman, but you've been 'round this bend with her before. So you finish watching the game while she goes on about how you need to be ready to go at 8:00 A.M. because Mr. Mitchell-or-something is going to be back to pick us up. *Yeah, right, hon. I'll believe it when I see it.*

You are asleep as soon as you get under the covers, but your wife keeps waking you up with her tossing and turning. Finally she gets out of bed, and you're dead to the world for another hour or so. *Good grief! Does she have to turn on every light in the house just to get dressed in the morning? Why is she standing in front of the closet like that? Next thing you know, I'll be hearing, "Honey, I don't have a thing to wear." Guess there's no use trying to get any more sleep around here.* So you throw on some clothes, gulp a bowl of cereal and sit down to tackle the checkbook. *Will this woman ever learn to control her spending? Will we ever get out from under the ridiculous interest rates on our credit cards? How can I stretch this paycheck to pay all these bills?* Tapping your pencil on the desk, you purse your lips and frown at the figures and vaguely hear your wife say something about going somewhere. It's Saturday and you don't remember having anything on your calendar.

Suddenly she's standing expectantly in the doorway with someone dressed like Ed McMahon. But the guy's cool—he hands you a new blue button-down shirt with a crested logo: MMTour. *Hmm, must be his business logo, kind of like the last golf tournament I played in.* And the next thing you know, he's got you in the back seat of his Hummer limo with all the hot coffee and bagels you could possibly want.

What on earth can be taking that woman so long? Wasn't she just here a second ago? We're keeping this guy waiting, and she knows how much I hate to make people wait for us. Why does she always do this to me? When she makes her appearance, you settle back, relieved, and enjoy the ride.

The limo rounds a bend in the road, and you're facing huge brass gates. *Your Marriage,* you read. *Unusual name.*

You slide out of the car and look around. Mr. Michaels says, "Welcome to your Marital Mystery Tour." All this stuff is yours and he's going to give you the keys after the tour. *Wow, not bad. Who did he say this belonged to before?* Something about a mystery, but you'll have to catch up on the details later. For now you just want to look around at all this land. *Bet I could make a killing with this place on the real estate market,* you figure.

"There is much more here than what meets your eye," Mr. Michaels continues. *Just as I thought—worth a bundle. I'll have to call an agent when we get home. I hope my wife is getting all the details. What's he saying about infinite?*

"Let us begin with the main house. Ah, here is the one." He slips a shiny key from its ring and holds it out to you. "This," he announces, "is the key of Comradeship."

As you reach for it, your wife steps between you and Mr. Michaels. "Well, you'd better give it to me," she says. "He loses everything." *Only my keys and my glasses and the checkbook. But why does she always have to act so superior? I'm not some stupid kid. And she loses stuff, too.* But she snaps the key onto her key ring and unlocks the door.

Alan and I set off across a grassy quadrangle at Colorado State University on a dewy June morning in 1974; Alan—as light on his feet as a gazelle—gliding across the turf, and I—lumbering behind him—gasping for breath in the thin mountain air. Why was I torturing myself this way? Oh, yeah. I was trying to stay in shape for gymnastics, and Alan was helping me. That's what friends are for.

A year later we entered into marriage with a solid friendship forming its foundation. Before our first date, we'd spent many hours together talking, studying the Bible, working out in the gym, hiking, and getting to know each other in a variety of situations.

Our relationship developed quickly. As new Campus Crusade for Christ staff members in training with Athletes in Action, we spent nearly every waking hour of the day in each other's company. From our morning jog, through three daily cafeteria meals, several seminary-type classes, an afternoon gymnastic workout, and evening study sessions, until our final "See you tomorrow," we were together.

We had been acquaintances in college, but beyond the gym, our orbits never intersected. Early in his freshman year, Alan had accepted Christ as his Savior and thrown himself wholeheartedly into Christian activities. He and several other likeminded gymnasts organized "Gymmies for Jesus" and performed in exhibitions to share God's love with their audiences.

That was my junior year. (Yes, Alan married an older woman.) The previous year (1970) I had been part of a group of students who had "taken over" the Administration Building. I had long, frizzy hair parted in the middle, and wore my dad's old Army jacket, bellbottom blue jeans, and a bra only when I absolutely had to.

But in February 1973, by God's boundless grace, and much to the dismay of my Jewish parents, I accepted Jesus as my Messiah. Grateful for my salvation and filled with zeal, I felt compelled to tell the immediate world how they could go to Heaven by personally receiving Christ.

When Alan learned the following spring that I, like he, was joining Athletes in Action, he called to encourage me. We, like other CCC staff members, were asking individuals and churches to sponsor us financially to attend the training in Colorado. I appreciated his emotional support since I'd been a Christian for so short a time and had relatively few contacts. Eventually, because we both lived in the East, we decided to share expenses and drive west together.

In the semi-hypnotic state induced by driving through Nebraska's cornfields, I recalled someone telling me during our college days that Alan was Jewish. At that time, I'd decided my source was misinformed because of Alan's involvement in Gymmies for Jesus. I'd thought no one could be Jewish and Christian at the same time. Now, however, I realized how possible it was, and I looked at my traveling companion in a new light.

Several months earlier, my friend Merry had suggested listing the qualities I desired in a husband so I could pray about it and recognize this man when he came into my life. My list consisted of 43 characteristics ranging from number one—Jewish background— through a well-rounded assortment of spiritual qualities—to number 43—six feet tall. I "placed my order" for a tall man of prayer, integrity, good humor and athletic ability with strong leadership potential. In other words, I didn't want to be able to push him around.

Now I turned to my comrade and asked, "Alan, you're Jewish, aren't you?"

Surprised by my question about his religious upbringing, he hesitantly responded, "Yes."

The realization hit me like a wet sponge. "Oh, no, Lord! Not Alan!" This definitely was not the man of my dreams. Why, he was only 5-feet-6! He didn't play the guitar or write poetry, and he had sloppy handwriting and about the worst spelling of any college graduate I had ever met! No, not Alan! Why, I was far too comfortable with Alan. He was like an old shoe. He was my *friend*!

Do you follow my line of reasoning? I had thought that in order to love a man, my stomach had to be so full of butterflies that I was practically nauseous! I had equated love with a tummy-turning emotion reserved for guys who aroused my sexual appetite and in whose company I felt perpetually flustered.

But Alan was my friend. He told silly jokes and made me laugh. He asked me deep, probing questions to draw out my thoughts and opinions, and then we'd argue about them. He saw me when I was all sweaty and covered with chalk from the gym, and I didn't have to primp or look perfect to impress him.

Webster's Students Dictionary defines comrade as "a chamber-fellow, companion, or associate." Derived from the Latin word for chamber, it evokes an image of an associate, someone joined with another in action or function, a colleague, a partner, an accomplice, a close companion. In marriage, a comrade is one who shares not only the bedroom, but also the boardroom, as a joint decision maker.

The word comrade reminds me of Bill Mauldin's Pulitzer Prize-winning World War II cartoons of two American GIs, Willie and Joe. They share the struggle to survive the agonies of war by sticking with each other through everything from boot camp to back home again. They meet each situation head on with humor and purpose, never wavering in their loyalty to each other. If Willie lags behind, Joe waits for him to catch up. If Joe loses some of his rations, Willie shares his. They're comrades, equals, working together for a common purpose.

How many of us view our marriage in this way? From "The Honeymooners" to "The Simpsons," the media has portrayed marriage as an armed truce at its best and all-out war at its worst. My generation grew up laughing at Ralph and Alice Cramden insulting each other, little realizing how destructive such a pattern can be for a marriage "made in Heaven."

If your marriage is missing the friendship factor, do not despair! In the next chapter, Alan and I suggest ways to build friendship into your relationship. Stop here first and "turn the key" in the "comradeship lock" by discussing the following questions with your spouse.

KEY-TURNING QUESTIONS

1. Whom would you consider to be a comrade in your life? What are the characteristics of that relationship?

2. Do you see your spouse as a comrade? If yes, in what ways? If no, why not?

chapter two

BUILDING A
FRIENDSHIP ROOM

LADIES FIRST

"Whoa! Can you believe this place?" your hubby gasps.

The two of you stand in the entrance hall swiveling your heads and marveling. Every detail of this mansion proclaims wealth and prosperity. Vaulted ceilings, polished marble floors, beveled glass windows—each architectural element reveals the designer's artistry.

Running a forefinger along the mantelpiece, you close your eyes and inhale deeply, relishing the sweet fragrance of the burnished wood. *Not a speck of dust anywhere. I wonder what the previous lady of the house was like. I'll bet she was really elegant.* You look at your hand on the wood and blush at the realization that your chipped nail polish and ragged cuticles don't exactly exude elegance. Thrusting your hands into your pockets, you continue exploring.

You find yourself drawn to one room in particular, not sure why. Everything about its decor, from the built-in bookshelves to the overstuffed loveseat invites you to make yourself at home. You kick off your sandals and wiggle your toes in the plush carpet, delighted by the way it caresses your feet until you look down and see that your toenails are in no better shape than your fingernails. Your husband has already wandered in and plunked himself down—legs stretched out, feet up—in a tan leather recliner. He smiles at you and sits up.

"Come on, hon. I challenge you to a game of checkers," he says, gesturing toward a game table next to his chair. "Remember how we used to play when we first started dating and didn't have any money to go out?" Soon you're engrossed in jumping his black checkers with your red ones, and he reaches across the table to take your hand murmuring, "I'd forgotten how graceful and soft your hands are."

"You've got to be kidding," you begin, remembering your neglected nails but blushing with pleasure all the same.

"You're so cute when you blush," he says. *Me? Cute? Blushing?* You're face does feel warm.

"Aha!" he shouts, jumping three in a row of your red pieces. "King me!"

"You stinker! No fair! You distracted me." And you grab a pillow from the loveseat to swipe at him, but he dodges and tackles you around the waist so you both tumble to the floor, laughing.

"This is the Friendship Room." Startled, you realize Mr. Michaels has been watching from the doorway. "The previous owners spent quite a bit of time here. As you may guess, it was their favorite room in the house."

AND GENTLEMEN

You stand in the entry looking at the place. *Rich, very rich people live in houses like this. It must cost a bundle in upkeep each month.*

You look around for a big, flat-screen TV and pool table and wander through a wide doorway into a most inviting room with an easy chair practically calling your name. There's no resisting the urge to sit—no, to lounge—in this room. *Mmm, good on the back, up go the feet.* It even has one of those vibrating chair cushions. *I could do this all day.*

Then you see the checkerboard. You haven't played in years. *She used to kick my butt at this game, but I learned that if I could break her concentration, I could usually win.*

"Come on, hon. I challenge you to a game of checkers. Remember how we used to play when we first started dating and didn't have any money to go out?"

The game starts out even enough, but soon you see her competitive edge sharpening as she plans how to double-jump your checkers. *I always loved how she throws herself wholeheartedly into a game, you think. There she goes, cranking up that thinly veiled urge to win. Man, I love that "go for the gusto" air about her. It sure turned me on when we first started dating.* But I can't let her win that easily.

You reach across the table to take her hand, saying, "I'd forgotten how graceful and soft your hands are."

"You've got to be kidding," she laughs,

There—she's dropping her defenses. Now if I can just get her to forget about this guy here in the corner . . .

"You're so cute when you blush." *Yeah, yeah, that a girl, forget that one; it's not important. Yes!*

"Aha!" you shout, jumping three in a row of her checkers. "King me!"

"You stinker! No fair! You distracted me." She swings a pillow at you, but your body still remembers your old football days and you easily duck out of her way, grab her around the waist (still so huggable after two kids) and pull her down—on top of you, of course. The sweet scent of her perfume and delectable softness of her curves fills your being with sweet longing to hold her closer as you both laugh like a couple of school-kids.

"This is the Friendship Room." *Whoa, how long has Michaels been standing there?* "The previous owners spent quite a bit of time here. As you may guess, it was their favorite room in the house."

⇌✦⇋

Alan and I were fortunate that our relationship began as a friendship. Although I thought I wanted a man who would make my heart skip a beat, I realized God knew better. What I needed was a comrade. Having begun in friendship, our relationship over the years has matured into a deep, enduring love.

What if your relationship began on the wrong foot? What if you and your partner were first united in lustful passion before you realized the consequences of such unstable underpinnings? What if the idea of being friends with your spouse has never occurred to you? Is it too late to try to rebuild this aspect of your marriage?

Friends of ours recently added a room to their house. Their home, which once adequately accommodated their family, seemed to shrink as the children became teenagers. The new addition opens from their dining room into a bright, spacious area full of windows and more than enough square footage to hold computers, video games, CD and DVD players and lots of teenage friends.

In the same way, you can build an addition onto your marriage relationship. If the "house" of your marriage is missing a "Friendship Room," it's not too late to add one. We want to give you a blueprint for adding a Friendship Room onto your marriage.

Through Alan's years of counseling people, we've found that a healthy friendship will go through five general phases: Superficiality, Testing, Exposure, Conflict, and Oneness.

Superficiality

Superficiality is that wonderful, early relational stage in which people discover all their similarities. ("Oh! You like Rum Raisin ice cream? No kidding! So do I!") Every shared taste or opinion is a cause for celebration, another confirmation that you belong together, that you're soul mates, and that your lives were meant to intertwine.

At this stage, finding things to do together is easy. Why, you enjoy doing practically everything together! You idealize each other, and there is absolutely nothing—or at least very little—that you would change about each other.

Testing

You determine to pursue the relationship further. You commit yourselves to each other in an exclusive bond (i.e. you "go steady," get engaged or even get married). Once this bond is established, the commitment is bound to be tested.

If you ever participated in scouting, you probably practiced tying knots. Square knots, overhand knots and half-hitches made up most of my limited repertoire of Girl Scout rope tricks. I was never great at knot tying, but one thing I remember (after "right over left and under, and then left over right and under") is pulling on the rope to make sure the knot would hold. I was testing the knot.

In a similar way, we test the strength of our commitment to one another to see if it can withstand a few strong tugs. What if you dare to disagree with him on an issue? What if you tell her you think orange is not her most flattering color, or you liked her hair better the other way?

I was looking for a strong leader and felt insecure when Alan started asking what I wanted to do on dates or how I thought something should be done. I was afraid of falling in love with a wimp and didn't want him to be too heavily swayed by my opinions (although I reserved the right to express them vociferously when I disagreed with his decisions).

I am also a map reader. I like to know where I'm going before I start out, so I know what to expect along the way—no surprises. Alan, on the other hand, learns how to get somewhere by getting lost first and finding out how not to get there. Moreover, I quickly learned that he (like many men) hated to ask directions. Somehow, stopping to ask an informed gas station attendant to get us back on the right track was an admission of defeat.

Believe it or not, I often wondered if I could be married to someone who became lost so frequently. I was highly critical of Alan's detours and wasn't sure I could accept this "defect" in his character.

Alan, on the other hand, soon became aware that I am habitually late. I maintain that it comes from growing up in a small town where nothing was farther than five minutes away. But whatever the reason, Alan had to decide whether or not he could bear to spend the rest of his life with someone who thought she could leave for an engagement at the same time she was supposed to be arriving there and still get there on time.

A crisis situation will bring out both the best and the worst in most people. Several months after Alan and I became engaged, we were in Pennsylvania visiting my parents and discussing wedding plans. Because of our Jewish families and our Christian faith, our wedding ceremony was becoming a touchy issue.

Alan thought he'd like a church wedding. His parents had no objections. However, my mother, who immigrated to the USA from Austria as a 14-year-old during the Nazi era, had an especially strong reaction to his plan. "Send me an invitation, and maybe I'll come!" she shrilled in a voice I had never heard before. Then she burst into tears—I had never seen her cry—and rushed from the room.

The following night, my grandmother suffered a massive stroke, her third, while watching TV in my parents' family room. We all stared aghast as the recognition and fear and, finally, resignation flickered in her eyes before she went limp. The paramedics were there in moments to take her away, and we were left in numb shock and sadness with the house still filled with the fragrance of the meal she had been preparing just minutes before.

Two days later, Alan and I went back to Chicago for a CCC Christmas conference, leaving my beloved grandma hovering between life and death, and my mother in a sort of armed truce with us. I called home after a couple of days, and my mother informed me that Grandma had died. When I asked her if she wanted me to come home, she brusquely replied that if I couldn't say *Kaddish* (the Jewish prayers for the dead) at my grandmother's graveside, then she didn't want me to come. And she hung up on me!

I was shocked and wounded by her rejection and cried for hours on Alan's comforting shoulder. Crying has never come easily to me, and I was embarrassed to allow my fiancé to see me with my drippy red nose and puffy red eyes. Yet Alan's acceptance of my appearance and encouragement to express my grief freed me to be honest with emotions I might otherwise have tried to smother. My natural tendency in that type of crisis situation had been to withdraw and wrestle with my feelings in private torment. But by staying doggedly by my side, Alan proved to me what a true and trusted friend he was.

We pooled our meager resources and bought a one-way ticket to Pittsburgh. I arrived home smothered in anxiety, afraid my mother would reject me totally. But when she saw me, she yelled, "Pauly's home!" and threw her arms around me as my dad came running.

That single episode did more to establish a solid foundation of trust in my relationship with Alan than any untested pledges of allegiance could possibly have done. He had come alongside me in my time of need and broken through the walls I characteristically built up around my emotions. I was grateful.

Exposure

In the course of time, a certain amount of exposure takes place. After all, you can't hide your true colors from each other forever, especially once you begin living together. Like the title of the old Clint Eastwood movie, you begin seeing *The Good, the Bad, and the Ugly* in each other.

Every so often, Alan would snap at me or overreact to something I said, or the way I said it. On visits with his parents, I noticed him reacting to his mother in a similar fashion. Because we lived hundreds of miles away and seldom visited his family, I hadn't witnessed this disrespect previously. The way he spoke to his mom on these occasions repulsed me, and I was offended that he would respond to me the same way. I didn't want to see such nastiness in my husband, but I had to accept that it existed.

I responded to those episodes with silent withdrawal, which Alan called "stewing." I didn't like his behavior, but rather than risk conflict by confronting it, I pulled into myself and pondered my critical thoughts. *How can he be that way? I would never act like that. If he really loved me, he would never talk to me that way.*

Over the next several weeks, Alan would have to coax the truth out of me, piece by obnoxious piece. I could really drag out my self-righteous, judgmental, withdrawal periods—Alan asks, "What's wrong, Pauly?" I respond, "Oh, nothing [sigh]."

As you see the rough edges, the "warts and all" sides of each other, you must consciously choose to accept this partner just the way he or she is. If you've not yet committed yourselves to each other, you must ask yourselves, "Can I live with this aspect of my loved one if my loved one never changes?"

Alan was especially irritated by my tendency to laugh when I was embarrassed or in any kind of emotional pain. The mixed messages confused him, especially if he was telling me that I had hurt his feelings in some way.

"Oh [tee hee]!" I'd giggle. "I'm so sorry [hee hee]. Really, I am [smiling]."

Thinking I was minimizing his pain and not taking his feelings seriously, he would become angry or frustrated with me. What he didn't understand was that I come from a family who dealt with pain by making jokes. His family, on the other hand, freely expressed all kinds of emotion in front of one another.

When Alan first told me about his fear of reading aloud in public, I (the honor student) was appalled. How could I, who derive tremendous pleasure from reading to others, be identified with someone who'd taken remedial reading classes in school and frequently loses his place on the page?

Alan loves to sing, but can never remember all the words to songs, so he makes up his own. This character "flaw" (according to me, the perfectionist) made me grit my teeth in our early days. I often corrected him until I finally realized that he would forget the same words again the next time, and decided I could choose to enjoy that he so often has a song in his heart.

Conflict

Eventually a relationship with any amount of honesty will experience conflict. Disagreements will occur because we're two separate people coming from different points of view and interpreting life's experiences through diverse grids formed by our backgrounds and personality traits.

If you never conflict with your spouse, at least one of you is lying or, possibly, withholding your true feelings. In a healthy relationship, both parties freely express their opinions without fear of risk to the relationship itself. For the first ten or so years of our marriage, I tried to avoid arguing with Alan at all costs—at least, out loud. Inwardly I carried on a running dialogue of things I felt like saying but was afraid to.

Unresolved conflict will result in a developing distance or emotional separation. Even though the pain of the emotional wounds you inflict upon each other will subside with time, without forgiveness and reconciliation, it is never totally forgotten. The next incident will call it right back up again, and the resulting separation will be greater than the previous one. Eventually the accumulated distance and wounding are so great, they seem insurmountable, and many couples decide to call it quits.

Oneness

However, with satisfying resolution (forgiveness and restoration—what Drs. John and Julie Gottman of the Gottman Institute call "repairing"), the conflict may actually result in greater oneness than the couple experienced initially.

The turning point came for Alan and me when we attended a communication workshop taught by Dr. Dallas and Nancy Demmitt, which equipped us with tools to "fight right," to verbalize negative feelings without bashing one another in the process. These skills gave us freedom to express our emotions, voice our opinions, and suggest possible solutions to our issues without escalating into a huge blow-up. We learned how to disagree without devaluing one another, to state an opposing position without jeopardizing our entire relationship. In fact, we learned what so many others in strong, vital marriages have learned—that when we disagree and work through our conflict to a mutually satisfying conclusion, our relationship ends up stronger than it was before. We experience the oneness that God desires for us.

KEY-TURNING QUESTIONS

Take some time right now to think about the following questions and discuss them with your spouse:

1. What (besides physical attraction) used to draw you together as friends?

2. What would you like to do now to help develop your friendship?

3. What are your individual interests? Where do they overlap? Discuss how you can develop a large area of overlap.

CONCLUSION

If your relationship has been devoid of friendship, it's not too late to start over. The Lord can redeem the time and "restore the years the locust has eaten" (Joel 2:25). Determine now to fashion a new beginning for your marriage based on the vital key of comradeship.

SECTION TWO:
The Key of Commitment

chapter three

WHAT IS COMMITMENT?

LADIES FIRST

Your tour of the house complete, you follow Mr. Michaels along a sun-dappled footpath through the apple orchard. *Why are we here?* you wonder. *Certainly there must be a catch somewhere. When is he going to give us the big timeshare pitch and ask us to sign away our life savings?*

Without warning, your husband bumps into you just as the path ends abruptly at a steep, rocky embankment. You stagger forward, striking your forehead on a jagged outcropping. *Yikes! That hurts!* Your hand flies to your head and you scowl at the smear of blood on your fingertips.

Without thinking, you react to the pain and embarrassment of the moment. "Is it too much to ask you to watch where you're going?" you demand, digging through your purse for a tissue or napkin or piece of scrap paper, anything to keep the blood from ruining your makeup and dripping on your sweater.

Your husband looks helplessly from your bruised and angry face to Mr. Michaels. The latter courteously removes a spotless white handkerchief from his breast pocket. "Please, allow me," he says.

Stepping forward, he dabs at the gash on your forehead. When he removes the handkerchief, your skin glows as healthy and pink as before the mishap. He folds the pristine white cloth and replaces it in his pocket.

"Now then, shall we proceed?"

You stare at Mr. Michaels and nod.

He reaches into his pants pocket and produces another key. "This is the key of Commitment." He hands it to your husband. "Look behind that rock," he directs, pointing to a mossy boulder. "You'll find the lock to your hillside vault."

Your husband stoops down, grunting, and fumbles around for a bit trying to get the key and the lock to cooperate with each other. He looks so inept and awkward. Whatever happened to the trim, virile athlete you married? Sometimes you feel embarrassed to be associated with him and feel torn between wanting to defend him and wanting to goad him into working harder to get back into shape. He's obviously struggling with getting the key to work in the lock. *Mr. Michaels must think he's so inept,* you think, increasingly self-conscious.

"What's the matter, hon? Too many thumbs?" you tease, hoping to sound lighthearted and ease your embarrassment. "Maybe it needs a more delicate touch."

"It's sticking. I can't turn it."

He sounds like such a whiner.

"Keep trying," says Mr. Michaels. "After all, this *is* the key of Commitment."

Your guide's words sting your conscience. *Whoa! What have I been thinking? I'm glad my husband can't read my thoughts like Mr. Michaels seems to do.*

AND GENTLEMEN

Your hormones were heating up in the Friendship Room, and you work at switching gears as you meekly follow Mr. Michaels out the door and down a winding path through an apple orchard. *Why does my wife look so unruffled? Wasn't she feeling anything back there when I was ready to lock us in the nearest bedroom?* Apparently she doesn't care about your physical desires as she strolls along chatting with that party pooper Michaels.

Glaring at your guide as you inwardly fume, you're unaware that ahead of you, your wife has halted, and you bump into her with enough force to knock her head into a jutting rock. In seconds a bloody gash erupts into a goose egg the size of Mt. Vesuvius above her left eyebrow, and you feel like dirt. You want to hide and hold her and call the paramedics and apologize all at the same time, but all you can do is stand there with your hands dangling at your sides while she reacts to the perceived insult.

"Is it too much to ask you to watch where you're going?" she chides, as though you're a child, and your desire to apologize chills as you brace yourself for a lecture. *Why does she have to sound so much like my mother in times like this? Does she think I'm a 2-year-old? I hate it when she talks to me that way.*

While you back pedal emotionally to escape her tirade, Mr. Michaels reaches into his breast pocket and produces a spotless white handkerchief (your grandmother used to lecture you on why you should always carry one). "Please, allow me," he says, and you'd think he was trying to kiss up to her if he weren't so genuinely sincere. You can't see what he does, but when he steps back, the huge, bleeding bump is gone. *Where did the blood go? Did I imagine this whole thing?*

"Now then, shall we proceed?"

You manage to nod.

Pulling another key out of his pocket, he hands it to you, saying, "This is the key of Commitment. Look behind that rock." He points to a moss-covered boulder. "You'll find the lock to your hillside vault."

Sounds easy enough, but your knees pop as you crouch down, and you have to be a bit of a contortionist to get your hand behind the rock. It's been awhile since you've had this type of exercise. *I sure hope there isn't any poison ivy or snakes back there,* you mutter to yourself, feeling around for a keyhole. But then, sure enough, camouflaged among the rocks and pebbles, you find the lock. The key slides easily into place but the lock seems to stick, and you jiggle the key, sweating with the awkward exertion.

"What's the matter, hon? Too many thumbs?" taunts your wife. "Maybe it needs a more delicate touch."

You feel your face and neck redden. Why do you put up with such mocking? She never talked to you like that during your dating days. *Where's the sympathetic smile and understanding nod she used to give me when I shared problems and concerns? What happened to that kind, understanding person,* you wonder. You think back to your first girlfriend and wonder if she's happily married. Maybe yours isn't a match made in Heaven after all. Plenty of your friends are divorced and seem to be enjoying the single life.

Now why can't I get this silly lock to open? "It's sticking. I can't turn it," you complain.

"Keep trying. After all, this *is* the key of Commitment."

Mr. Michaels' words sting your conscience. *Whoa! What have I been thinking? I'm glad my wife can't read my thoughts like Mr. Michaels seems to do.*

⋙⬥⋘

Blood brothers . . . soul sisters . . . kindred spirits . . . "*agape*" love. These words summon images of undying devotion—the Indian boy and the settler's son cutting themselves with a pocketknife and laying their open wounds across each other to share blood. (These days with AIDS, who would risk that?) Anne of Green Gables and her beloved Diana. Han Solo and Luke Skywalker. Jesus and His disciples. You and your spouse?

In my post college days when I was searching for ultimate Truth, I often took long walks with my brother's dog, Tigger. Tigger and I trekked along the rambling streets and roads of my hometown. Occasionally, I stopped to visit a friend or go into a store. No matter how long I stayed inside—a few minutes or a couple of hours—Tigger was waiting for me when I came out. Tigger was faithful.

three: What Is Commitment?

Each summer when Alan went to summer camp, the entire camper population was divided into two teams for "color war." One event involved approximately twenty boys from each team: Standing in line, each boy had to reach one arm between the legs of the boy to the front and the other between his own legs to the boy to the rear.

The whole "chain" shuffled backwards, lay down on their backs, then all stood up to shuffle across a goal line, hopefully without breaking the chain. Although quick and strong, Alan was so small they called him "Mighty Mouse." The other boys tightly gripped his clenched fingers and he theirs. Sometimes his feet would come entirely off the ground while he held on to avoid breaking the chain. Sometimes his hands would be bloody from his teammates' fingernails digging into his flesh. But Mighty Mouse would not break the chain. For an 11-year-old, that was commitment!

Gymnasts learn new moves with the aid of "spotters." A spotter catches a gymnast to break his or her fall in case he or she misjudges a landing or the amount of rotation or speed required to successfully complete a skill.

I remember standing at one end of a black rubber runway looking at a sidehorse that seemed a mile away and a mile high contemplating my handspring vault. My coach, Miss Mimi Murray, stood like a tower of strength and confidence to launch me over the gargantuan obstacle in my path.

Would I run fast enough? Would I end up on the right foot the right distance from the springboard? And, most importantly, would Miss Murray make sure I made it over? The thought of crashing into the sidehorse was always a powerful deterrent to taking off down the runway.

Finally I would go for it and run full-tilt down the black mat. If I didn't run fast enough, I wouldn't have enough momentum to make it over the horse, so once I made my decision, there was no turning back. *Okay, Mimi, into your hands I commit my body.*

Eleven quick, pounding strides were all it would take to reach the springboard. *Both feet hit the board . . . hands up over the head . . . tight gluteus . . . drive the heels . . . and YES!* Miss Murray's capable hands on my pelvis for a little extra *oomph,* and I'd be flying through the air like Peter Pan! For one brief, weightless, heady moment defying gravity! Wow! What a rush!

But I never would have experienced the thrill of completing the vault, if had not decided to commit myself to Miss Murray's coaching. In this context, the word commitment carries the idea of trust in another person, believing he or she will not fail to carry out some duty or obligation toward oneself.

When Jesus was dying on the cross, He cried, "Father, into Thy hands I commit My spirit!" With these last words, the Son of God entrusted Himself totally to the care of His Father, knowing that God, who promised redemption for all mankind through the sacrifice of His Son, would not fail or forsake Him in His hour of darkness.

Commitment also may mean a pledge, a promise, a vow, or a contract, as committing oneself to finish a certain task or job. In marriage, the weight of the word increases with the idea of a covenant. According to Gary Inrig in his book *Whole Marriages in a Broken World,* a covenant differs from a contract in several ways.

While a contract involves an exchange of services or goods for some type of payment in return, a covenant entails a mutual vow "by a person to a person." Just as God promised Israel that He would be their God and they would be His people, so a husband pledges himself to his wife and she to him.

Inrig states, "So the marriage contract does not read, 'I, Gary, take you, Elizabeth, to be cook, companion, housekeeper, and sexual partner.' I entrusted my *self* to her and she entrusted her *self* to me. That is the essence of marriage as a covenant. 'I, Gary, take you, Elizabeth.'"[1]

---

[1]Inrig, Gary, *Whole Marriages in a Broken World* (Grand Rapids, MI: Discovery House Publishers, 1996), p.54.

A covenant is also public—visible to all—permanent, unconditional and binding, involving trust and grace. Inrig writes, "Covenants are high-maintenance items. They require continual attention to sustain their vitality."[2]

In a faith-based marriage, our first commitment in every sense of the word must be to the Lord. In Romans 12:1, the apostle Paul strongly urges all believers to "present [our] bodies a living and holy sacrifice, acceptable to God, which is [our] reasonable service of worship." Many well-intentioned couples enter into their nuptial vows riding on a wave of emotion and blinded by the stars in their eyes. They think the strength of their love for one another will be enough to carry them through the trials of life without considering that God calls them each individually first to a commitment to Himself.

Our commitment to another person begins when we see in that person something that promises to meet our expectations for a life-long relationship. But that human commitment may disintegrate like a sandcastle in high tide if our expectations fail to materialize.

Our ultimate commitment to our spouse originates in the Lord's commitment to us. "We love, because He first loved us" (1 John 4:19). Before we even existed, Jesus Christ committed Himself to die for us, not only as a sin offering and an example of sacrificial giving, but also to leave us His Holy Spirit's power to draw upon in our commitment to each other. Only in His Spirit do we have the power to love unconditionally and permanently and to keep the promises of commitment we have made to each other.

---

[2] ibid., p.58.

KEY-TURNING QUESTIONS

1. Have you ever made a commitment of your life to the Lord? If not, see the Appendix to learn how you can begin life's most exciting adventure.

2. How would you describe your commitment to your spouse?

3. If you need to reaffirm your commitment to your spouse, look him or her in the eyes and complete the following sentence: "I, _____, confirm my commitment to you, _____, based upon the Lord's commitment to me and mine to Him."

4. Describe a time in your life when you made an unreserved commitment to a person, task, or cause, and share it with your spouse. Now apply that feeling to your relationship with your spouse.

chapter four

HOW'S YOUR SERVE?

LADIES FIRST

With a slight rumbling, the hillside shifts, and a section of what had appeared to be immovable earth swings outward. Without thinking, you grab Mr. Michaels' arm for support and you're amazed at the sudden surge of strength and well being you feel. He smiles down at you, and a memory of Daddy kissing your boo-boo flashes through your mind, warming your soul. *When was the last time I felt this secure with my husband,* you ask yourself.

Now the earthen door swings outward, and you gasp as it reveals a surprisingly large, well-lit room within the hillside. Awestruck, you look up at Mr. Michaels, half expecting to see your father's face. "The lights come on automatically when you open the door," he explains.

"Hey, hon, give me a hand, will you? I dropped the key, and I can't find it." Your husband's voice jolts you back to the realization that he's sitting indecorously on the ground, blindly patting the pebbles behind the mossy rock. Feeling a bit exasperated with his ineptitude, a sarcastic putdown springs to your mind, but before the words can form on your lips, Mr. Michaels says, "It's just a bit to the left of your thumb."

"Got it!" Your husband scrambles to his feet and follows you inside the cavern. Although you know you're standing in a cave, the room's appearance belies its location. Ivory-toned walls reflect soft, recessed lighting. Plush carpet, antique mahogany end tables, brocade wingback chairs and life-sized portraits in gilded frames provide an air of subdued elegance.

We've never been able to afford these kinds of furnishings, you fret. He always insists my desires for some of the finer things in life are too materialistic, as if I'm totally self-centered and greedy. He sure doesn't mind spending money gratifying his own desires—nights out with the guys, season tickets for basketball, golf. So why does he begrudge me a few simple pleasures in life? You'd think it was totally extravagant to . . . Your thoughts trail off as a framed photo strikes you as familiar, and you move closer to examine it. Just then, from across the room your husband shouts (way too loudly), "Hey, hon! Look at this! It's that picture of our family reunion from last Christmas! I wonder how it got here."

"That's impossible," you reply, striding over to him. Then, "Oh my gosh! You're right! How strange." You find yourself looking for clues in the back of Mr. Michaels' head. But your mysterious host has moved across the room toward a gated doorway.

He turns to face the two of you and says, "This vault is built into a hillside. The only entrance is behind you, and you hold the only key. It also unlocks the gated doorways to each of the storage rooms. Riches beyond your dreams are stored within this cavern, and they are all yours. But you must unlock each gate and take possession of what is yours. Enjoy it, my friends."

AND GENTLEMEN

Suddenly the key meshes with the pins and turns inside the lock. Squatting awkwardly on your haunches, you feel the ground vibrate with a slight rumbling, and the hillside shifts, knocking you off balance and onto your rump. From that vantage point, feeling a bit like Indiana Jones, you watch an earthen door swing open. You look away from the cave's surprisingly well-lit interior and are scanning the hillside for hidden cameras when you realize you've dropped the key.

"The lights come on automatically when you open the door," says Mr. Michaels, and you glance up to see your wife hanging on his arm, gazing tenderly into his face. *Now what? Is she flirting with this guy just because he wears an expensive suit?* Swallowing your jealousy, you say in your most casual, nonchalant tone, "Hey, hon, give me a hand, will you? I dropped the key, and I can't find it."

She lets go of Mr. Michaels' arm and starts toward you with that look on her face that she usually reserves for toddlers with messy diapers, when Mr. Michaels says, "It's just a bit to the left of your thumb."

Oh, give me a break, Mr. Mind Reader. Sure enough, there it is. "Got it!" you proclaim, scrambling to your feet and following them inside, feeling like your wife's kid brother tagging along on her date. But once inside, you forget about those unmanly feelings. Whoever would have guessed that this spacious room lay hidden inside this hillside? And how on earth does all this stuff work? You start poking around the walls, looking for ducts and outlets and thermostats, when a framed photo catches your eye and you move closer to examine it. That group of people looks just like . . .. "Hey, hon! Look at this!" you call to your wife. "It's that picture of our family reunion from last Christmas! I wonder how it got here."

"That's impossible," she replies in that clipped "teaching voice" of hers. Then, "Oh my gosh! You're right! How strange."

Now how did Michaels come up with all this personal stuff, you wonder. *He's certainly done his research. So now what? Is he going to tell us we're on "Candid Camera" or in a television soundstage like Jim Carrey in* The Truman Show?

But Mr. Michaels simply turns toward you and your wife and says, "This vault is built into a hillside. The only entrance is behind you, and you hold the only key. It also unlocks the gated doorways to each of the storage rooms. Riches beyond your dreams are stored within this cavern, and they are all yours. But you must unlock each gate and take possession of that which is yours. Enjoy it, my friends."

~~~

As important as it is to love your spouse, your first love must be for the Lord. The primary commandment will always be "And you shall love the Lord your God with all your heart, with all your soul, with all your mind, and with all your strength" (Matthew 22:37). Next comes, "And you shall love your neighbor [read, your spouse] as yourself" (Matthew 22:39).

Our human tendency is to think your partner will meet your expectations. But you cannot avoid letting each other down in some ways. In those disappointing times, your commitment in the Lord holds you together.

Paul exhorts us in Colossians 3:23, "Whatever you do, do . . . heartily, as for the Lord rather than for men." Whatever you do, whether in your role as husband, wife, child, parent or employee, you are to serve God in your service for others. Make no mistake— marriage is full of service to your partner. Even so, whether serving is your spiritual gift, or if you, like me, would rather be waited upon, your service is first of all to the Lord.

Early in our marriage Alan labeled me a "Jewish American Princess." I couldn't understand why he would say such a thing just because I kept asking him to hire me a housekeeper. After all, my mother always had one.

When I was a child, if I got sick, my mother made up the couch for me in the den by the TV. There I would lie in regal misery, watching TV or reading or coloring. Occasionally Mom would wander in and ask if I wanted some ginger ale or chicken soup. Otherwise, I was left blissfully alone. On the rare occasions when I get sick as an adult, I pretty much like things the same way.

When Alan gets sick, however, he wants my company. He wants me to drop what I'm doing (forget the laundry, housecleaning, grocery shopping, ironing, and cooking), sit at his bedside and soothe his aching brow. (At least that's the way it seems to me; he says he just wants ten minutes of my time.) The occasional ginger ale or chicken soup is not enough. He wants me to serve him. That type of service is so foreign to my natural, inherently selfish makeup, the only way I can do it is as unto the Lord.

In your marriage, who will take out the garbage when the trashcan starts to overflow? Who is going to get up at 2 A.M. to see why the baby is crying? Who will clean up the dog's messes in the back yard? Who will run to the store when you run out of milk? Who's going to make the bed? Or even help make the bed? Who gets to clear the table? Who will help get the children ready for church so you can all arrive on time?

We are to follow the example of the Lord Jesus Christ Himself who "did not come to be served, but to serve" (Matthew 20:28). According to Ephesians 5:21, husbands and wives are to be subject to one another in the fear of Christ. "Impossible!" you may be saying. "You don't know my spouse. You don't know how demanding and unappreciative he/she is. You don't know how hard it is to serve someone like him/her."

All true, I'm sure, just as it's often true of me and of Alan. But Jesus came not only to show us a better way, but also to give us the power to live it out. Read on.

KEY-TURNING QUESTIONS

1. On a scale of 1 to 10, what is your commitment to serve your spouse?

2. Describe three ways you demonstrate unreserved service to your spouse. If you don't, what would it take for you to start serving? Hint: If this is a weak area for you, ask your spouse what he/she appreciates about your service. Ask how you could serve him/her better.

Note: Many times we serve others the way *we* would like to be served rather than the way *they* like to be served. In that case, we are serving only ourselves. Be sure you serve your spouse in a way that truly meets his/her needs.

chapter five

SO WHAT IF I'M NOT A PERFECT 10?

LADIES FIRST

Your mouth begins to water and your palms feel sweaty in a decidedly unladylike way as Mr. Michaels precedes you to the gated doorway. *Riches beyond my dreams,* reverberates through your mind. *What would I do with that?* You mentally review recent issues of *Lucky, Better Homes & Gardens, Architectural Digest* and *Harper's Bazaar,* where just a simple skirt can cost $1,000 and a minor home improvement project might run more than the value of your entire home. *But if we had unlimited resources, I could spend as much as I want on clothes, and never have to even think about a budget,* you think. Names starting with "V" like Valentino, Vuitton and Versace spring into your mind. Forget K-Mart, or even Macy's. *I could shop in specialty stores where they don't even put price tags on things because people who shop there can afford everything.*

Just then, Mr. Michaels turns toward you, and his piercing look stabs your conscience. *Of course, if we had that much, I'd give plenty to the church, too.* You quickly amend your thoughts (as though your host is reading them) to include all the missions organizations and worthy causes you'd generously contribute to, even the public radio station. But as he turns his attention toward your spouse, a resentful little voice in your mind brings up all your previous dates and romances. *Maybe one of them might have provided for me in the way I really deserve, and I'd never have had to struggle to budget my hard-earned dollars to afford a few of the finer things in life.*

Now, despite your efforts to appear nonchalant and relaxed, you begin grinding your teeth, clenching and unclenching your jaw as you and Mr. Michaels wait for your husband to unlock the gate.

"Go ahead, try your key. It will work," Mr. Michaels says, prodding your husband out of some sort of reverie. He looks (somewhat stupidly, you think) from your host to the key in his hand.

"Come on, honey, wake up!" you say, grabbing the key from him and inserting it into the lock. The gate glides open, and you all step inside. *What riches will we now possess?*

Nothing could have prepared you for the display of "wealth" that greets you. The room is filled with memorabilia—well-loved dolls and plush animals, dog-eared baseball cards, Legos, Play-Doh sets, Matchbox cars, Star Wars Jedi-knights light sabers, just-like-mommy's makeup sets, video games—all the toys of your childhood.

"Oh my gosh!" you cry, surveying the room. "Can you believe this?" You pick up a Barbie doll wearing sunglasses and a bathing suit. "I had one just like this, except it had a crayon mark where my little cousin tried to color the back of its . . ." You close your mouth as you find the purple dot on the calf of the doll's right leg.

Your husband, engrossed in a Nintendo game, ignores you, and you're drawn to another item. "I remember when my cousin and I built a kite just like this one and flew it in the field across the street from our house," you say to no one in particular. "The grass came up to our knees, and the wind blew just right for the kite to fly up, it seemed like to the end of the stratosphere. That was a perfect day!"

You're vaguely aware of your husband's voice saying, "I remember the first time I saw one of these games. The ways that mushroom gave people superpowers seemed magical to me." But turning toward his voice, you catch a glimpse of familiar, yellow book jackets—Nancy Drew mysteries! A bookcase full of them against the far wall. Soon you're absorbed in *The Case of the Whispering Statue* and memories of swapping books with your sixth-grade classmates.

When Mr. Michaels taps you gently on the shoulder, you jump.

"Would you like to see another room?" he asks.

"Yes, of course." You drag yourself back to the present. "Where's . . .?" Mr. Michaels points to your husband, sitting cross-legged, bent over a comic book in the opposite corner. You smile at his little-boy posture, and he looks up at you, grinning.

"My mother said comics were a waste of time and money," he says. "But that didn't stop me from collecting Batman and Spiderman issues. These are just like the ones I used to have. Come take a look."

As you start toward him, you see Mr. Michaels watching you and remember his invitation to view another room. Now you feel self-conscious and embarrassed about keeping your host waiting, so you snap, "Grow up and get a move on, hon. We're keeping Mr. Michaels waiting."

His brow furrows, but he gets up and follows you to the next gated doorway, where Mr. Michaels asks, "Where is the key?"

You glare at your husband as he stutters, "Th-the k-key? Uh, what did I do with it?" You look away, pursing your lips and shaking your head as he digs in his pockets. Now he looks at you. "Didn't I give it to you?" he asks, and you want to shoot him for trying to pin his ineptitude on you. *Why can't he just focus on one thing at a time and keep track of his stuff?* Finally, he runs back through all the places you've just left, and you cross your arms and follow him, scanning every surface beneath tightly knit brows.

"Mr. Michaels said this was the only key. What will we do if he's lost it? How can we ever replace it?" you mutter to yourself. You remember when your husband misplaced another key, one to a friend's vacation home, and you thought not only would you have to spend a night out in the cold, but it would cost you that friendship.

"Ah, but he'd given your friends' key to you for safekeeping, and you had it in your purse all along, didn't you?"

What? Surely that was Mr. Michaels' voice, but he's standing in the doorway, gazing intently at something all the way across the room. Still, now that you think of it, he's right—everything did work out in that situation, and you were grateful your husband never mentioned it again.

"Maybe you could be a bit more gracious, too."

What's that? Mr. Michaels' voice again, but he's turned away from you. Whether you heard his voice or not, you realize you've been too critical of your husband and determine to change your attitude. And here he comes, waving the key aloft. "Here it is!" he calls to you.

"You look like a kid who got out of detention early," you say, smiling, hoping he picks up on the "warm, fuzzy" vibes you're sending.

"The funny thing is," he says, ignoring your quip, "I was never in the part of the room where I found it. It was on top of a bookcase full of old Nancy Drew books. I wonder how it got over there."

A sudden stab of realization pierces your smug bubble, and you remember grabbing the key and unlocking the gate and considering putting the key on the key ring, then getting sidetracked by the Nancy Drew books. You know you need to apologize, but your husband continues, "See, I'm not the only one who loses things. You don't have to act so darn superior all the time. You make mistakes, too. After all, I *am* the man of the house, and you owe me a little respect."

Relief, embarrassment, and defensive pride jockey for position within you. Pride wins.

"I'm sorry, dear—all right? But I don't need a lecture. Just hand me the key, and I'll put it on the key ring with the first one."

"All right, Madame Know-It-All. But don't try holding on to it with your magnetic personality, 'cause it's not working." And you both burst out laughing.

AND GENTLEMEN

Riches beyond my dreams . . . riches beyond my dreams. Wow, I could pay off the mortgage, get a place at the beach, and a boat and a Mercedes or a Lamborghini or both, you think as you follow Mr. Michaels to the gated doorway. You glance at your wife's intent features framed in the barred opening. *We never seem to be satisfied anymore no matter how much we have or what we do. Our life feels flat and colorless. Well, maybe if we're rich, we can be happy.*

You wonder sometimes if things would have been different if you'd waited and not been in such a hurry to get married. But she was so "hot" and your hormones were raging and her folks were pressuring you and the timing just seemed right. Still . . . maybe one of your former girlfriends might possibly have been better suited for you. If you'd married one of them, would that spark of romance still ignite the fires of passion in your heart?

"Go ahead, try your key. It will work." Realizing Mr. Michaels is addressing you, you grope your way back through your thoughts to the present. You look from your host to the key in your hand.

"Come on, honey, wake up!" snaps your wife, grabbing the key from you and opening the gate.

The room looks more like a giant neighborhood yard sale than a cache of treasures. Toys, books, bicycles, dolls, video games . . . *Video games? What's this? It's my very first Nintendo with the Super Mario Brothers game! I'll bet I still remember where all the magic mushrooms are.* Soon you're absorbed in the adventures of a little cartoon man hopping over turtles and fiery lakes. Now if you can just keep his superpowers long enough . . .

Your wife's voice floats dreamlike across the room saying something about kites. But you're enthralled in your own memories. "I remember the first time I saw one of these games," you tell her, intent on the game. "The way those mushrooms gave people superpowers seemed magical to me." But, glancing up, you see she's ignoring you and has walked away.

Well, if that's the way she's going to be, I can ignore her, too. Hmm, what else is there to look at here? Holy cow, Batman! A whole pile of superhero comic books! And all my favorites, too.

Eventually, you look up to see your wife smiling at you and think how much you enjoy that smile and her company, too, when you're not bickering. "My mother said comics were a waste of time and money," you tell her. "But that didn't stop me from collecting Batman and Spiderman issues. These are just like the ones I used to have. Come take a look."

She starts toward you, but abruptly her mood changes. "Grow up and get a move on, hon. We're keeping Mr. Michaels waiting." Now why did she have to go and spoil such a friendly moment by talking down at you?

Reluctantly you follow her to Mr. Michaels standing in the next doorway. He asks, "Where is the key?"

Good grief, not the key again? What's that thing made of, butter? you wonder. *It sure seems hard to hold onto.* You feel around in your pockets, muttering, "The key? Uh, what did I do with it?" Sneaking a glance at your wife, you see her glaring at you, lips pursed, shaking her head with that all-too-familiar "why am I married to such a child" look.

Aha! Now you remember. "Didn't I give it to you?" you ask her. But she just gives you a disdainful look, and there's nothing left to do but retrace all your steps, while she stands there, arms folded in impatient judgment. Nope, not at the comic books, not at the Nintendo station. Feeling helpless, you look over toward Mr. Michaels, but he seems to be staring at something cattycorner across the room from you. What on earth could he be looking at? Following the direction of his gaze, you arrive at a case full of yellow-jacketed books. And on top of it—the key!

Relief! Retribution! Revenge! Righteous indignation! You grab the key and, holding it aloft, stride back across the room toward your wife.

"You look like a kid who got out of detention early," she says.

But you've had enough of her smart little quips. "The funny thing is," you say, "I was never in the part of the room where I found it. It was on top of a bookcase full of old Nancy Drew books. I wonder how it got over there."

You watch the smug expression on her face melt away. "See, I'm not the only one who loses things." You're starting to get wound up and know she deserves every bit of what you want to say to her. "You don't have to act so doggone superior all the time. You make mistakes, too. After all, I *am* the man of the house, and you owe me a little respect."

For a moment she looks like she's going to apologize. But then you see her stiffen, and what she offers seems more of a brush-off than an apology.

"I'm sorry, dear—all right? But I don't need a lecture. Just hand me the key, and I'll put it on the key ring with the first one."

Suddenly you've got the perfect comeback. "All right, Madame Know-It-All. But don't try holding on to it with your magnetic personality, 'cause it's not working." *Thank God I can still make her laugh.*

⋙✦⋘

As couples embark on their Marital Mystery Tours, they are bound to encounter locked gates blocking their progress. The key of Commitment unlocks many of those gates.

The first major gate many couples confront is *lack of physical acceptance.* In this era of sexual "freedom," many couples enter into marriage having already overstepped the boundaries God designed for our health and safety. I assume, however, that at least some of you, like Alan and I, waited until your wedding night to totally disrobe in each other's presence.

No matter when the occasion occurred, at some point you stood before each other like Adam and Eve in the garden. But were you, like they were, "naked and unashamed?" Or did you inwardly shudder over the exposure of some real or imagined physical flaw?

On our wedding night Alan shuffled meekly into the bathroom where I was undressing and asked if I could accept his body. I looked at his wonderfully toned gymnast's muscles and thought,

63

"What is there not to accept?" We were both athletes with maybe a few ounces of body fat between us, yet we felt insecure about our imagined imperfections.

My friend "Jill" has told me how her husband and father-in-law used to make fun of her expansive hips. Even when she was young and fashionably thin, with sparkling brown eyes, lustrous hair, a bright smile, and a multitude of other attractive qualities, her husband undermined her fragile self-esteem by attacking her at the weakest point of her self-concept.

I didn't realize until after Alan and I were married (and he told me) that I had bad breath. *Aaghhh!* The scourge of every commercial-watching baby boomer! Morning mouth! Dragon breath! We would be sitting in church, and I'd be singing hymns in joyful abandon, when he'd slip me a breath mint. Or else he'd lean over and tenderly whisper, "Do you have any gum?"

Oh, no! I'd think. *Who was the last person I spoke to? Did I knock her dead with my breath?*

Then I'd get upset with Alan for having the nerve to expose my flaw. Finally, though, I was grateful to him for loving me enough to clue me in and do what he could to help me improve my halitosis. After all, he's the one who kisses me good morning each day.

As I mentioned earlier, I had always wanted to marry a tall man. Although Alan had a wonderful physique—broad, powerful shoulders and a slender waistline—I had trouble accepting his height, or rather, lack of it. When we walked together by plate glass windows, I was afraid to look, imagining myself to be towering over him. I'm only five-feet-two, but in the early 1970s, young women wore platform shoes with 4-inch heels. I felt like a giant, even though in my tallest shoes, I was still shorter than Alan.

I had to come to the point where I could look at Alan and say, "Yes. Lord. This man is perfect for me. You made him exactly the right height for me. I accept him just the way he is."

The truth is, we all have things about ourselves that we have trouble accepting: a large nose, a pock-marked complexion, frizzy hair, short legs, flabby thighs, male-pattern baldness, prominent ears, crooked teeth, and so on. When I don't accept one of my physical traits, my tendency is to assume that my partner doesn't accept it either.

Alan and I have learned the value of verbalizing our acceptance of each other. "Honey, you're just right for me." "I love everything about you." "You're just the right size." "I think your _____ is perfect just the way it is." "I know you're trying to lose weight, and I appreciate that because I think it's better for your health, but I love you no matter how much you weigh." These are all examples of ways you can encourage your spouse and express your commitment to him or her in the physical area.

We have friends—both men and women—who have gained more than forty pounds since they've been married. Some women gain weight with their pregnancies, others with menopause, still others as a side effect of various prescription medications. Some people eat for comfort. My gynecologist informs me that it's normal for women to gain three to five pounds with every decade over the age of thirty. And according to the Mayo Clinic Web site, most women gain about a pound per year in the years leading up to menopause.

The apostle Paul counsels Timothy that "bodily discipline is only of little profit, but godliness is profitable for all things, since it holds promise for the present life and also for the life to come" (1 Timothy 4:8). People naturally tend to focus on their physical attributes because they are so tangible, so visible. Yet you must remember that your body, like the grass of the field, exists here on Earth only temporarily; it will soon return to the dust. It is far more important to concentrate on developing within yourself and encouraging in your spouse the growth of eternal qualities within the soul.

KEY-TURNING QUESTIONS

1. What, if any, physical attributes do you not accept in your-self? In your spouse? List them.

2. Are you able to change any of these characteristics? If yes, what will you do about them? If not, are you willing to give up to God right now the things you cannot change and give thanks for the way He has uniquely made you?

Note: As you went through this chapter, some painful issues may have surfaced, which cannot be resolved through the simple exercises in this book. In that case, we strongly encourage you to seek the help of a trained Christian counselor, pastor, or other mature believer in Christ.

chapter six

IS THERE A RIGHT WAY
TO BE ME?

LADIES FIRST

Still chuckling, you accompany Mr. Michaels into the vault's next room, a gallery containing your family histories—photo albums, diaries, transparencies, super-8 movies, videotapes and DVDs. State-of-the-art computer equipment projects 3-D displays of your forebears welcoming you to your biographical library.

"Where did he get all this stuff?" you whisper to your hubby. Glancing at Mr. Michaels you say, "Do you think he's with the FBI or something?"

"Honey, your imagination works overtime. Why can't you just take what he told us at face value? He said he was representing the interests of the estate we inherited, and that's that."

"But something weird is going on. He knows too much. Have you noticed how he seems to know our thoughts?"

"What are you talking about? I think you're just spooked because this whole thing is out of your control."

And you're such a control freak, you read in the imaginary cartoon balloon above your husband's head.

"Excuse me," Mr. Michaels politely interjects. "Would you like to see the virtual reality presentation?"

After donning headgear and wired bodysuits, you enter the worlds of your past. Surrounded by the sights, sounds, even smells of your ancestral homelands, you walk the paths and cobbled streets of the generations that preceded you.

No wonder we approach things so differently, you think. You hail from generations of rugged farmers eking out existence on small plots of rocky soil. Their fierce independence and fiery tempers defied all authority, even as it gave them the strength to tame the uncooperative land on which they lived. He comes from a long line of scholars and intellects with a family tree bearing the fruit of knowledge fertilized by teachers, researchers, and college professors for generations. Real adventure for modern members of his family consists of writing the winning grant proposal. Your side of the family, meanwhile, yearns for excitement and chafes against the restraints of civilized monotony.

Suddenly you see the resemblance between yourselves and the diverse roots of your family tree. There's his great-great grandfather playing chess wearing the same intent expression you just saw on your husband during his video game. Great Grandmother tastes the chicken soup and Grandma looks for her reading glasses and mutters to herself while Grandpop tinkers in his workshop. *These family patterns are really engrained*, you realize. *And I thought I could change my honey once we got married—ha!*

"Time to move on," Mr. Michaels announces. "Who has the key?"

"I do," you say, patting your purse. "I decided if I put it immediately on my key ring, I'll never misplace it. A good system, don't you think, hon?"

"Sounds like a good plan, honey. All you have to do is follow through and do it, just like sticking to a budget."

AND GENTLEMEN

Relieved that you were able to get your wife to laugh, you move on with confidence into the next room, a technophile's dream. Up-to-date video equipment flashes displays portraying your family histories. And you used to think history was boring! You were never able to keep all your great-greats and cousins straight, but here they are—or at least, their projected images are—telling you all about their lives and loves and gains and losses. Finally, you can see where you got your hairline.

The 3-D hologram projection of your great-uncle reminds you of Princess Leia's image saying, "Obi-Wan Kenobi, you're our only hope." And you're just about to ask Mr. Michaels if he's borrowed some technology from Stephen Spielberg, when your wife asks you, "Where did he get all this stuff? Do you think he's with the FBI or something?"

What is it with her? You swear you'll never understand how her mind works. "Honey, your imagination works overtime. Why can't you just take what he told us at face value? He said he was representing the interests of the estate we inherited, and that's that."

"But something weird is going on. He knows too much. Have you noticed how he seems to know our thoughts?"

"What are you talking about? I think you're just spooked because this whole thing is out of your control."

And you're such a control freak, you think, glad that she can't read your thoughts.

"Excuse me," says Mr. Michaels. "Would you like to see the virtual reality presentation?"

As he fits your wife with headgear and a wired bodysuits, you lean in and ask, "Where did all this hi-tech stuff come from? It seems like your outfit must have some connections with Hollywood or the Pentagon or something. Have you got a special deal with some higher-ups somewhere?"

"Higher-ups? I suppose you could say that," answers Mr. Michaels. "But if you'll just hold your questions until the end of our tour, I'm sure they'll all be answered along the way."

For as complicated as the bodysuit and helmet are, they're amazingly light and flexible. *Fits like a glove,* you think. You admire the way your wife's outfit hugs the contours of her body and wonder how soon it will be before your tour takes you to a bedroom and if you can get Mr. Michaels to give you some privacy there. But then you're transported through the worlds of your ancestors. Watching how hard they work, you gain a new appreciation for modern conveniences and wonder how any of your forbears had time or energy for sex. But then again, sex doesn't really take all that much time if you just do a "quickie."

Hey, there's Michaels walking along a cobblestone street. What's he doing here in my virtual past? Before you have time to dwell on that thought, you enter a Victorian-style house and see your great-great grandfather engrossed in a chess game. You feel his excitement as he captures his opponent's castle. *Just like Super Mario making it past that lake of fire.*

Whoa! And who's that? Don't tell me that's my wife's great grandma with her nose in a pot of chicken soup. She and my wife could be twins!

This experience has certainly given you a new appreciation for your families' differences. She comes by her independent spirit naturally with all those tough pioneering farmers in her gene pool. And you never realized how much of your intellectual curiosity and love for games and puzzles was inherited. No wonder you enjoy the challenge of writing grant proposals but, unlike your wife, gain no satisfaction from coaxing flowers and vegetable to grow in the uncooperative soil of your back yard.

"Time to move on," Mr. Michaels announces. "Who has the key?"

"I do," pipes up your wife; *a bit too proudly*, you think. "I decided if I put it immediately on my key ring, I'll never misplace it. A good system, don't you think, hon?"

"Sounds like a good plan, honey. All you have to do is follow through and do it, just like sticking to a budget."

⇒◆⇐

This "gate" in our tour leads us to the area of your *personalities*. How would you describe your personality? Are you outgoing, cheerful, boisterous, candid, bold—or shy, withdrawn, serious, introspective, reflective, inhibited? These traits are as distinctive as our noses.

Alan and I have two sons, Josh and David, born twenty months apart. We used to call them "Mr. Night" and "Mr. Day." From the very beginning, their personalities were opposites.

Josh was born squalling and yammering following ten hours of hard labor. We could almost imagine him demanding, "All right, who decided to pull me out of my nice, warm, comfortable womb? I'm cold and wet, and it's all YOUR fault!"

My labor with David, on the other hand, lasted only three hours, with no hard contractions. He just kind of slipped out, calmly looked around and seemed to say, "If you could each please tell me your name and what your function is here, I would certainly appreciate it."

Now well into adulthood, Josh and David retain their distinctly different personalities, reflected in their interests, lifestyles, and career choices.

Alan and I, like many couples, possess opposing tendencies in our personalities. I tend to be the "thinker." I analyze movies and study the motivations of the characters. Alan is the "feeler." Movies that manipulate our values and opinions hit him hard in the emotions, and he's upset by the way Hollywood can portray evil as good.

I love to read fiction and appreciate the craft of writing, the way words "sound" to me as I read them and the joy of a well-crafted novel. Alan, on the other hand, wants to read practical "how-to" books and counseling-related nonfiction.

When I read the Bible, I'm fascinated by words and their shades of meanings, and the lives of its heroes and villains and how various concepts relate to one another. Alan always wants to know, "So how does this apply to your life?"

I'm a detailed person, always trying to tie up loose ends and finish off projects neatly. Alan is conceptual, going for the big idea, leaving loose ends all over the place (makes me crazy!)

I'm a night owl. He's a morning person.

I'm habitually late. He's very prompt.

I tend to be indirect and tactful in discussing problems. He takes a much more direct approach—going for the jugular, I say.

When we were in school, I crammed for exams, got A's and then promptly forgot the material. Alan was a C-student, but continues to apply what he learned.

I follow directions to the letter. He doesn't even read directions.

I don't want to make mistakes. He learns by making mistakes.

I meander through my day, moving from task to task, working on several projects simultaneously (very inefficient). He makes his schedule, prioritizes his activities, and follows through on his objectives.

We have learned that there are strengths and weaknesses to both sides of our differences. My penchant for details means I do things "right." But I also take a long time to get anything finished and tend to procrastinate. Alan plunges in and gets the job done, even if it's not to my picky satisfaction. I have had to admit that sometimes, just getting it done is enough.

We have discovered three "gate openers" in the area of personality differences.

1. *The need for humor in recognizing your differences.* We can choose whether to become irritated over our divergent approaches to life or to laugh with each other about them. Just as we've learned to joke about Mr. Night and Mr. Day, we can laugh at Mrs. Detail and Mr. Concept. Alan has learned to give me 5-minute (or 10-minute or half-hour) warnings when we need to get ready to leave in order to arrive somewhere on time. By accepting my tendency to putter until it's too late, and *gently* reminding me of the time, Alan has defused this "time bomb" in our relationship.

2. *The need to not set up oneself as the standard and point to the other's differences as "wrong."* My tendency to stay up late and putter is no more or less correct than Alan's early morning bursts of energy. Alan places a high value on arriving at our destinations ahead of schedule; I value coming home to a house that's in order, and it's worth taking the time before we leave to clean up the kitchen or put away the stacks of laundry on the living room sofa.

The wife who is always at the center of a laughing group of people at a party is no more "right" than her husband who's engaged in intense one-on-one conversation in a corner of the room. His ability to restrain his tears is no more "right" than her crying at the drop of a hat (or a teacup from Grandma's set of china.)

Our human inclination to measure all personality traits against our own must die on the cross with Jesus and be resurrected to newness of life in Him. He is our standard, yet the Bible says little about His human personality traits, which leads us to our third point.

3. You need to know and accept that God created each of your personalities uniquely. He made me just the way I am, complete with a tendency toward melancholy and introspection. He designed me with an eye for detail and a love of laughter. He's not surprised that I hate lima beans and adore chocolate chip cookie dough ice cream; that I cry at sad movies and laugh at Bill Cosby. He knew before the beginning of time that I would fret for weeks over a mistake in the checkbook. And He is somehow glorified when I can accept all these idiosyncrasies about myself, give Him thanks for making me just the way I am, and release myself with all my imagined irregularities into His hands to be remolded for His service.

Moreover, He is further glorified when I accept some very dissimilar irregularities about my husband. Who am I to tell the Master Potter that He goofed in crafting His masterpiece? "The thing molded will not say to the molder, 'Why did you make me like this,' will it?" (Romans 9:20). I have an obligation to the Lord not only to accept, but also to be grateful for the way He designed my personality as well as Alan's. Anything less than that is idolatry (setting up myself as more of an authority than the Lord Himself).

KEY-TURNING QUESTIONS

1. Which gate opener do you need the most?
    ❑   I need humor in recognizing our differences.
    ❑   I need to not set up myself as the standard and point to my spouse's differences as "wrong."
    ❑   I need to know and accept that God created each of our personalities uniquely.
2. How can you further develop this area in your marriage?

3. Identify two personality differences you have trouble accepting in your spouse. How can you apply your chosen gate opener to this trait in your spouse?

chapter seven

AVOIDING THE "ALWAYS WARS"

LADIES FIRST

Even as you unlock the gate to the next room, the warm, sweet scents of cinnamon and pine and the tinkling bell tones of Christmas carols waft out. Icicle lights frame the entrance to a shimmering wonderland of twinkling bulbs and pine garland, and a 16-foot silver spruce under the vaulted ceiling displays ornaments remembered from childhood, as well as from your tree at home.

Someone with enormous creativity and patience has decorated a half-dozen tables with the colorful, familiar motifs and symbols of seasonal holidays. Softly illuminated Chanukah menorahs and traditional Passover plates seem perfectly at home alongside Easter baskets and lilies, Mother's Day bouquets, Thanksgiving cornucopias, and birthday cakes.

"Are those real presents underneath the tree," your husband asks, "or just artfully wrapped empty boxes for decoration?"

You're about to snap back, "What kind of question is that? Didn't I get you enough last year," when Mr. Michaels takes your arm and guides you across the room toward a presentation on HDTV. *Good-*

ness gracious, there's the surprise sleepover party Mom threw for me in fifth grade! You never truly appreciated how much work and creativity she put into planning family events. But now you see her addressing invitations with "SHHH!" written in bold letters on the envelopes. And there she is stringing crepe paper and blowing up balloons and decorating your cake and greeting your girlfriends while you're on a contrived errand with your dad. No wonder you love making such a big fuss about your kids' birthdays.

Every holiday and event is the same way, celebrated to the hilt with pomp and pizzazz. And there's . . . *Oh my goodness!* You point at the screen, yelling over your shoulder, "Look here, hon! That's my favorite uncle!"

"You don't have to yell, dear—I'm right here." Your husband's voice is subdued.

"Oh, sorry, hon. I didn't realize you were so close. I just got so excited seeing my sweet uncle again. It was my turn that year to buy his present. We always exchanged names at Christmas so we wouldn't go broke buying a bunch of cheap, meaningless gifts for the whole family."

"Really? Well, as you know, we decided when I was a kid to forego presents at Christmas altogether and donate the money we would have spent to a local orphanage. Then we gave one another other gifts of service, like doing their laundry or helping with math homework."

"Oh. So now we're playing Whose Family Had the Most Meaningful Christmas, are we? Why do you always have to win every point in every discussion?"

The color rises in his neck. "Honey, I'm not trying to compete with you. I was merely trying to explain what my family did."

But you've stopped listening. You turn to the sparkling room and ask no one in particular, "What would Christmas be without presents?"

AND GENTLEMEN

Getting in that final quip about the budget felt satisfying. *She thinks she's so competent because she can make things grow in her garden, but for crying out loud, does she have to overspend on it every month? She's forever buying seedlings or fertilizers or mulch or something for that plot of dirt out in the backyard.*

She unlocks the gate to the next room and you stand blinking at the holiday displays, hit by a tidal wave of conflicting emotions. Christmas carols, twinkling lights, birthday cakes, Thanksgiving turkeys, red and white Valentine hearts, even Chanukah menorahs and Passover plates—the scene overwhelms your senses.

And the huge decorated tree in the middle of the room . . . That wrapped gift looks just like the one you envisioned when you wrote to Santa the year you turned nine. You could never ask your parents to get you an automated Battleship game, but maybe Santa would bring you one secretly if he knew how badly you wanted it. You weren't so sure Santa existed anyway and thought you'd give him one last try.

Of course, I didn't get it.

"Are those real presents underneath the tree," you ask Mr. Michaels, "or just artfully wrapped empty boxes for decoration?" But your host appears not to have heard your question as he takes your wife by the elbow and guides her to another part of the overdone holiday room.

You begin to perspire, feeling stuffy amid all the symbols of holiday hype. *So that's it—Michaels brought us here to guilt us into buying a bunch of stuff at his gift shop. Yeah, sure, it's the All-American way to capitalize on people's guilt and fear of never giving enough to make others feel special. So every celebration is about spending more and more money. Well, I'm sure not going to get sucked into a gigantic marketing scheme to put my hard-earned dollars into some gigantic corporation's pockets just because they start promoting Christmas shopping in July.*

Where's my wife? I've got to get her out of here before she whips out her credit card and buys half the store.

There she is across the room staring at another one of those high-tech video displays. *I hope she's not expecting me to buy her an HDTV next. I'll bet that's what Michaels is selling. I'd better go make sure he's not talking her into ordering one.* And you start walking toward her.

Just then Mr. Michaels speaks softly into your ear (*Wasn't he just across the room with my wife?*), "We're not trying to sell you anything, you know. All this is already yours."

You're about to protest your innocence regarding such thoughts but realize that somehow he would know you're lying.

"And you know, no matter what's inside that box under the tree," Mr. Michaels continues, "your parents loved you very much."

Your eyes and throat start to burn and you're about to ask what he knows about your feelings toward your parents. But now you're next to your wife, who turns her head over her opposite shoulder and yells, "Look here, hon! That's my favorite uncle!"

You clear your throat and swipe at your eyes, saying, "You don't have to yell, dear—I'm right here."

"Oh, sorry, hon. I didn't realize you were so close. I just got so excited seeing my sweet uncle again. It was my turn that year to buy his present. We always exchanged names at Christmas so we wouldn't go broke buying a bunch of cheap, meaningless gifts for the whole family."

"Really? Well, we decided when I was a kid to forego presents at Christmas altogether and donate the money we would have spent to a local orphanage. Then we gave each other gifts of service, like doing each other's laundry or helping with math homework."

"Oh. So now we're playing Whose Family Had the Most Meaningful Christmas, are we?"

You feel the color rise in your neck. *Ouch, that hurt. Why does she always have to throw those sarcastic barbs?* "Honey, I'm not trying to compete with you. I was merely trying to explain what my family did."

But she's clearly stopped listening. She turns away and says, "What would Christmas be without presents?"

A third gate consists in the *habits and patterns* we bring into our relationship. Each of us comes from a unique family background with its own history and established ways of approaching life. Even people coming from similar neighborhoods and socioeconomic status must deal with the differences in their family upbringings.

As we mentioned earlier, Alan and I are both from Jewish families, yet our religious experiences are very different. His family members are Reform Jews, who rarely attended religious services, while I was reared in a Conservative Jewish tradition and once wanted to be the first female rabbi.

Additionally, my mother's Holocaust experience caused her to cling to her faith like a "Titanic" survivor to a life raft. I grew up eating kosher meat and loving the traditions and celebrations of the holidays. Every year we kept the custom of refraining from leavened foods (bread, cereal, pasta) for all eight days of Passover (or Pesach), not just the first night when most Jews have their *seder*, the ceremonial meal that marks the beginning of the holiday and retells the story of the Exodus from Egypt. There was something awful and mysterious about the Ten Plagues culminating in the slaying of the firstborn, which the Israelites escaped by slaughtering a lamb and painting the doorposts of their homes with its blood as a sign so the angel of death would "pass over" it.

I thrilled to the ritual of my dad holding up a piece of *matzoh* (the unleavened bread) while he led us in the recitation of liturgy from the *Hagaddah* (literally "the telling"), "Lo, this is the bread of affliction." Then he would break the matzoh and wrap half of it in a napkin to become the *afikomen* (or dessert), which he would later hide. After dinner, all the children would search for the afikomen, and whoever found it would get a dollar. My first "aha" moment of identity with my ancestors came during one of these seders as we recited the words, "We were slaves in Egypt." I, in the form of my ancestors, had once been a slave, but the God of Israel had set me free! I had no idea at that time how much of a slave to sin I was.

Alan says his family "celebrated Christmas and Chanukah, and had the best of both holidays" (meaning lots of presents). His religious education was an addendum tacked onto his life out of obligation by parents who no longer practiced their faith. They ate ham and other non-kosher foods and belonged to a private Jewish country club. My family's social life revolved around the easy informality of the Jewish Community Center and our tightly knit group of Jewish friends. My family ate in the kitchen; Alan's in the formal dining room. I spent two weeks of my summers at a local Girl Scout camp. He went to an eight-week all-Jewish sports camp in New Hampshire. My dad sold life insurance in a coal-mining community in southwestern Pennsylvania. His dad commuted to New York City and traveled to Europe dealing in semi-precious gems.

When I first met Alan's family, their large house and material wealth intimidated me. I was afraid of using the wrong fork or saying the wrong thing or dressing improperly. I was fearful Alan would expect me to cook like his mother and present five-course meals served on silver platters every night.

Because most of us live for eighteen years or so with at least one, if not both, of our parents, our family traditions become pretty ingrained. Even things that we may not consider traditions *are* in practice.

Does your mother *always* wash and save her aluminum foil?

Does the dog *always* stay outside?

Does your dad *always* carve the turkey?

Did you *always* open your Christmas presents (a) the night before Christmas, (b) first thing Christmas morning, (c) after Christmas dinner?

Did your father *always* read the newspaper when he got home from work?

Did your mother *always* fix you lunch?

Did she *always* have milk and cookies waiting for you when you got home from school?

Did your mom *always* do all the cooking (and cleaning and laundry)?

Did your dad *always* take out the garbage?

Did he *always* wash the car and make sure it was filled with gas and functioning mechanically?

Can you see how these "always" areas are sources of potential conflict in your marriage? Or how your expectations of your roles may be based not on a biblical model but on a familial one?

"For this cause a man shall leave his father and his mother, and shall cleave to his wife," stated the Lord God in Genesis 2:24. Jesus repeated these words in Matthew 19:5 and Mark 10:7, and the apostle Paul reemphasized them in Ephesians 5:31. To merit so much repetition, this idea of "leaving and cleaving" must be very central to a successful marriage.

Leaving father and mother involves more than just moving out of your old bedroom at your folks' house. Each newly married couple must establish their own identity as a separate unit from either of their families of origin. To remain financially or emotionally dependent on parents is like the ancient Chinese practice of foot binding. Just as the Chinese wrapped tight bandages around their young daughters' feet to prevent them from growing unfashionably large, so financial or emotional dependency upon parents will prevent the healthy development of a marriage.

Not only are couples to leave their parents' homes, they are also to cleave or cling tightly to one another. Alan and I have heard psychologist and author Dr. John Trent tell the story of his father fighting in the trenches during World War II. After clinging desperately to his rifle throughout the night, his fingers would become frozen in position around his weapon. No longer consciously gripping his rifle, his hand was now *cleaving* to it.

This picture demonstrates the determination with which you are to forge your identity as husband and wife, one flesh. You must take the various distinctive qualities and expectations you each bring into marriage and consciously determine how to meld them into a relationship that is more than equal to the sum of its parts.

In chapter 2, I mentioned the conflict over our wedding plans. I wanted a traditional Jewish ceremony, but no traditional Jewish rabbi would agree to officiate. Alan wanted a church wedding, but that idea offended my mother. Our pastor suggested a third alternative, unique to ourselves, a civil ceremony. We wrote our own vows based on Scripture, and a friend sang "The New Twenty-third Psalm" and Noel Paul Stokey's "Wedding Song."

My mother helped me pick out the gown and the invitations. My dad paid for everything and walked me down the aisle. Our sisters cried. My grandfather lifted his hands over us and pronounced the Aaronic benediction, a traditional Jewish blessing. With God's guidance we were able to create a ceremony and a day of celebration meaningful and joyous for all.

Over the years we've developed some traditions of our own.

Alan *always* opens the car door for me. (I've learned to sit and wait for this one.)

We *always* kiss each other hello and good-by.

We *always* hold hands and pray before meals, even in public.

We *always* spend Thanksgiving with Alan's family.

We *always* visited my family in Pennsylvania for two weeks during the summer (before my dad died and my mom moved into assisted living).

We *always* read a new version of the Christmas story when we got home from church on Christmas Eve and opened one present with the children before they went to bed.

Alan *always* gets me strawberry pie for my birthday.

I *always* got a "surprise" breakfast in bed on Mother's Day (until the kids moved out and I told Alan I'd just as soon forego the "honor").

We *always* put little clues on the outside of our Christmas presents to help each other guess what's inside while wrapping them to be misleading.

Sometimes you may not even realize that something was an unwritten tradition in your home until you find yourself saying, "My mother (father, family) *always* did it *this* way."

Like your personalities, your family traditions and the ways you approach life are embedded in the "skin" of your souls. You can't just rip them out of your spouse without doing a lot of damage. You need to recognize and accept these differences without judgment. Just because one of you expects every occasion to be a cause for a huge celebration while the other doesn't, that doesn't make one of you the "good guy" and the other the "bad guy." With open, honest, loving communication, the two of you can decide what traditions are right for you.

KEY-TURNING QUESTIONS

1. List and discuss habits, patterns, and traditions that you enjoy and desire to keep in your marriage.

2. List habits, patterns, and traditions brought from your family of origin that are a source of conflict within your marriage. Discuss ways to resolve the conflict and form your own new traditions.

chapter eight

HOW EFFECTIVE IS YOUR UMBRELLA?

LADIES FIRST

For the moment, the holiday room has lost its allure. You've always loved creating as close to a magical feeling as possible for the honoree at every occasion. Little birthday girls become princesses wearing tiaras and feathered boas and rhinestone-covered plastic high heels. And birthday boys get to be superheroes or Jedi knights or whatever their hearts desire on their special day. Didn't you just go all out planning a surprise party with two-dozen guests for your husband's birthday?

And Christmas . . . don't get you started on Christmas. You shop the post-holiday sales to get the best buys on decorations for the following year so your house can become an even more wonderful Christmas wonderland. Perplexed by your husband's bewildering criticism of the way you try to make such occasions special for your family, you walk away muttering to yourself.

Christmas without presents? No wonder we have so much conflict over how much to spend on gifts for the kids. I knew he was always pressuring me to volunteer at a soup kitchen or something for the holidays, but why didn't we ever talk about his "no presents" thing before? I would have understood, wouldn't I? I had other boyfriends and we were always able to talk about stuff like that.

Soon you're reminiscing about those old high school romances and how different, how much easier, how much more romantic life would now be if only you'd married your first true love. He was so good-looking and you used to get butterflies in your stomach when he caught your eye in the hall between classes. You remember the delicious thrills of excitement you felt when he held your hand for the first time, and the giddiness of dancing with him at the prom. You certainly don't feel those giddy tingles anymore when your husband gives you "that look" as you're undressing for bed at night.

Splashes of pink, blue, yellow, and orange light spilling onto the floor from a doorway ahead remind you of that idyllic prom night. You peek inside expecting to see pastel-colored paper lanterns casting their glow. Instead you find a grotto filled with umbrellas in a vast array of styles and designs. Prints, plaids, and solids in every color are suspended from the ceiling and covering the walls. Tall folded golf and beach umbrellas lean against one corner, while a fringed patio umbrella shades a round table and matching chairs in another.

Baffled, you turn to look for Mr. Michaels, only to find him and your husband right behind you. "You never know when a sudden shower will spring up around here. They pass quickly, but you want to be protected, so you don't get drenched. The previous owners always carried an umbrella just in case. You'll probably want to do the same thing."

AND GENTLEMEN

Stung by her lack of compassion, you watch your wife walk away muttering to herself.

Doggone her, you grumble inwardly. *She doesn't know what it was like being the only kid on the block who never had a new bike or toy to show off after Christmas. But my folks were afraid I'd become too materialistic and selfish if I didn't learn to give to others less fortunate. Doesn't she know how much it hurt or how embarrassing it was for me? Why can't she just accept me the way I am like my secretary does? Not only is she competent, she really respects me and hangs on every word I say.*

"You know, when she walks away from you like that and you close your heart toward her, she's left uncovered and vulnerable to spiritual attack."

"Mr. Michaels?" you ask. Surely that was his voice just then, but where is he?

"Ah, there you are," says your host, approaching you from beyond the Christmas tree. "I've been meaning to talk to you about umbrellas. Do you know what they are for?"

"Well, sure," you reply, not sure where this conversation is heading. "They keep you dry when it's raining."

"That's right. They're a form of protection from the elements, not just rain, but also, at times, the sun and its harmful ultraviolet rays. You know it's interesting about the sun—its light is an absolute necessity in our world, but direct exposure to it for too long can burn one's skin or cause cancer. Yes, an umbrella can protect you—so long as you have one with you, that is. The problem is, when the weather is fine, most people don't carry one even if they have one.

"Come along," he continues, walking toward a rainbow-colored ray of light pouring out of a doorway.

"Did you ever think of yourself as a sort of umbrella for you wife?" he asks. "You can cover her from the storms of life, but you have to be available to do that, and she has to be willing to let you. Right now it appears as if she's a bit uncovered."

Your wife turns around as you approach her, and Mr. Michaels says, "You never know when a sudden shower will spring up around here. They pass quickly, but you want to be protected, so you don't get drenched. The previous owners always carried an umbrella just in case. You'll probably want to do the same thing."

Even if your wife doesn't get it, you know he's not talking about the weather.

THE SPIRITUAL AREA

Scripture warns Christians against marrying nonbelievers. Yet even Christian spouses are not guaranteed to be of equal commitment to Christ or maturity in the Lord. This inequity may lead to problems, especially if the less mature spouse is the husband.

Women tend to express a wider range of their emotions and, thus also, their praise to God more freely than men do. They often have more time available for Bible studies and small groups, building their confidence to pray aloud and discuss spiritual things. A very vocal woman may inadvertently overshadow and intimidate the husband she wishes would take spiritual headship in their home.

Often a man who is reluctant to pray aloud with his wife believes she will judge his lack of eloquence or fervency or sincerity. And what if his prayer isn't answered according to his desire? He may imagine her ridiculing his lack of power or criticizing him for being out of touch with the Spirit of God.

The male ego is fragile. While we ideally seek to humble ourselves in the sight of the Lord, no man wants to appear ridiculous before his wife. Think about it, ladies. Has your husband ever attempted to lead out in Bible reading only to have you brusquely correct his pronunciation of a hard name or tell him how much you already know about this passage? It doesn't take much for him to decide, "I'm never gonna do *that* again."

Or perhaps you've asked him to pray about a problem you're facing, and he comes to you with what he believes is God's leading. Maybe it's not the answer you wanted to hear. Do you begin backpedaling and seeking other answers elsewhere, or do you give him the opportunity to take spiritual headship in your home in a practical way?

The issue here is no longer his relative maturity, but your trust. Do you trust God enough to lead you through this man whom you've vowed to love, honor, and obey?

Alan has always been a strong spiritual leader in our home, a quality for which I prayed specifically in my list of 43. I'm grateful for the strong spiritual covering he has provided for our children and me, and over the years have learned the danger of stepping out from under the protection of his headship. Like the big red umbrella that's the logo of a major insurance company, Alan's spiritual covering protects me from Satan's attacks and many of the world's temptations, and provides a sense of security and safety and blessing shared with him.

I've found that when I grow critical of him and his decisions, or rebellious and inwardly angry and resentful of his leadership, I "poke holes" in that umbrella or toss it aside altogether. This leaves me exposed to life's storms and unprotected from the "roaring lion" who constantly "prowls about . . . seeking whom he may devour," according to 1 Peter 5:8. In my life, these attacks begin in my thought life with vain imaginations ("What if I'd never married him in the first place?") and a roving eye ("So-and-so certainly is handsome. I wonder if he thinks I'm pretty.") Left unchecked and unconfessed, these types of thoughts could eventually lead to actual infidelity.

Even if your husband's spiritual umbrella is full of holes, he is still the covering God has provided for you. Paul wrote to the Corinthian church in 1 Corinthians 11:4-16 that women should pray and prophesy with their heads covered, a symbol of their need for spiritual covering. In some churches, women cover their heads with hats or scarves during worship. Although this practice is not an imperative of Scripture, I believe wives must be aware that God has provided their believing husbands as their spiritual authority.

Clearly, it is imperative that "the wife see to it that she respect her husband" (Ephesians 5:33b). In other words, no matter how little he appears to pray or study the Bible, no matter how spiritually inept he seems to be to his wife, the husband *is* God's spiritual authority in the home.

If you are not happy with the condition of your umbrella, your best course of action is to pray, *pray*, PRAY and to trust, *trust*, TRUST.

KEY-TURNING QUESTIONS

1. Does one of you feel inadequate in the spiritual area?

2. How can the more mature of you encourage your spouse's spiritual growth?

   a) Wife, ask your husband how you can encourage him as the spiritual leader of your home.

   b) Husband, ask your wife what she would like to see you do as her spiritual covering.

Remember, *no blaming or criticizing!* This exercise should be a positive experience.

When you are finished talking, kneel together and pray for each other's spiritual growth.

chapter nine

FORGIVING WHAT IS PAST

LADIES FIRST

Still puzzling over Mr. Michaels' remarks about the weather, you follow him toward a doorway dancing with glimmers of light. Inside, bright reflections emanate from hundreds of mirrors on the walls. Frames of all sizes and styles—from ornately gilded to basic pine—border the silvered glass.

What a fascinating room, you think as hundreds of your reflections mimic every move you make. Remembering a hand mirror your aunt gave you as a gift, you scan the walls until you spot it among a collection of similar designs. Somehow, you knew it would be there.

Your husband waves at you from the Star Wars corner. "Look, hon! I had this one by my bed when I was a kid. One day my cousin and I were horsing around in my room with a football. I threw him a pass, but my aim was a bit off, and he missed and the ball went straight into that mirror. What a crash! I thought my mom was going to shoot us."

Sounds familiar, you think, picturing the porcelain figurine that lost its head when he and a buddy decided to bat around one of the kids' Nerf balls in the living room. Now that you think about it, very few of your figurines are still intact. *When will this guy ever grow up?*

"How interesting," you manage to respond, coolly.

"What is it with you, O Great One? Are you the only person who can get excited about this stuff? You can ooh and ah over your stuff, but I can't be . . . excited too?"

"Come on, hon, grow up. You're behaving like a child."

"No, you're the child, dear, a self-centered, self-, a self- . . ." he splutters.

Mr. Michaels materializes between you and takes you each by the hand. Surprised by his sudden appearance, you allow him to lead you before another mirror that stands alone in a private niche— a cross, outlined in teardrops of crimson rubies.

"The previous owners called this vault The Forgiveness Room," Mr. Michaels says.

You echo, "The Forgiveness Room?"

And your husband asks, "Why?"

"See that mirror in the shape of the cross?" Mr. Michaels answers. "Take a closer look at the inscription at the foot of the cross."

He draws your hands together and gives you a slight push forward. Hand in hand you approach the cross and read the following words:

Look in the mirror and what do you see?
Remember your human frailty,
And when you are hurt by another's sin,
Recall the reflection you've seen herein.

AND GENTLEMEN

Yeah, the weather, you think. *She sure has created a lot of storms along the way. I will never understand how a person who can be so charming and engaging and helpful and funny and loving one day can turn into a total witch three weeks later. And, for crying out loud, it happens every month! You'd think she'd learn how to control herself one of these days. Heck, once a month I'm the one who needs an umbrella . . . to keep the poison darts from hitting me in the head.*

You follow your wife into a room full of mirrors. They're displayed on the walls as if you're in a furniture warehouse, according to some system of categories you're trying to figure out when you spot the Star Wars corner.

Don't tell me . . . As if you half-expected it, there's the very Luke Skywalker mirror you and your cousin shattered into a zillion pieces with a football while pretending to be Joe Montana in your bedroom. You felt totally devastated. Your folks thought the mirror was a frivolous purchase, yet you'd saved all your lawn-mowing money for weeks, even doing extra chores around the house to get it. You couldn't cry in front of your cousin, so you just pretended to laugh it off and made jokes about what a juvenile mirror it was anyway, and how you'd grown way beyond the Star Wars stage. If your cousin had ever seen you cry, he'd never let you live it down. Maybe your wife will understand how you felt about it. She knows how bad it feels when stuff breaks.

You wave her over. "Look, hon! I had this one by my bed when I was a kid. One day my cousin and I were horsing around in my room with a football. I threw him a pass, but my aim was a bit off, and he missed and the ball went straight into that mirror. What a crash! I thought my mother was going to shoot us."

But she just gives you one of those "grow up" looks and brushes you off with an icy "How interesting."

Whoa, that sure takes the wind out of your sails. "What is it with you, O Great One?" you fume, as hurt reverts to frustration and frustration to anger. "Are you the only person who can get excited about this stuff? You can ooh and ah over your stuff, but I can't be . . ." Flustered and agitated, you search for the right word, then finish lamely, " . . . excited too?"

"Come on, hon, grow up. You're behaving like a child." *Ooh, she can be so snooty.*

"No, you're the child, dear, a self-centered, self-, a self- . . ." you splutter.

93

Part genie, part babysitter, Mr. Michaels materializes between you and takes you each by the hand. Surprised, you let him steer you to another mirror that stands alone in a private niche—a cross, outlined in crimson ruby teardrops.

"The previous owners called this vault The Forgiveness Room," Mr. Michaels says.

Your wife echoes, "The Forgiveness Room?"

And you say, "Why?"

"See that mirror in the shape of the cross?" Mr. Michaels answers. "Take a closer look at the inscription at the foot of the cross."

He pulls your hands together and gives you a gentle shove forward. Hand in hand you approach the cross and read the following words:

Look in the mirror and what do you see?

Remember your human frailty,

And when you are hurt by another's sin,

Recall the reflection you've seen herein.

⋘❖⋙

True commitment requires learning to accept and forgive each other's *past issues*. My "wild and woolly" college days made this a difficult area for Alan and me. I had been fairly promiscuous, and my resulting shame and guilt drew me to the Lord.

When Jesus entered my life with His love and forgiveness, He washed me clean, made me new. Like the woman in Luke chapter 7 who bathed Jesus' feet with her tears, I loved Him much because I had been forgiven much.

For a year after my conversion, I didn't date as I learned to love my Christian brothers with Christ's pure and holy love. When Alan and I married two years later, I viewed myself as a virgin in Christ, even though I recognized that physically I could never reattain that status.

Alan knew in general about my past. But on our honeymoon he began probing for details. As he expressed his shock and hurt over the extent of my promiscuity, I felt betrayed and wounded by what I perceived as his rejection. I thought our marriage was over just as it was beginning, and felt doomed to a union with a man who couldn't accept or forgive me.

Eventually we worked through our feelings and fears, yet Alan's initial reaction undermined my trust in him. I developed a reluctance to open up to him about my sins of the flesh. Not until we learned the communication skills we'll present in the next chapter was I able to fully discuss and resolve this issue with Alan.

We all need forgiveness.

Without forgiveness, unresolved conflicts create holes in the fabric of your marriage. Such holes don't fix themselves. If you don't properly mend them, those holes never go away. They continue to accumulate, weakening the fabric until it tears completely. Yet even as you might continue to wear a pair of blue jeans despite a torn pocket, having a few tears in your marriage relationship doesn't necessarily spell its demise. You learn to work your way around the fragile spots and try not to draw too much attention to them.

However, the negative effects of conflict *without forgiveness* are cumulative and progressive. As unresolved incidents add up, they intensify in their ability to damage various areas of your relationship. Without forgiveness, a couple grows progressively more distant from each other until hope for reconciliation seems totally lost. Sadly, at this point a large percentage of couples both in the world and in the church decide that continuing the relationship is not worth the effort or the pain, and they split up.

But God has provided us with both His example and His atoning, cleansing blood to wash us clean. He gives a fresh start to all who come to Him in faith. Just as we so hungrily receive His love and forgiveness for our own offenses, so we are exhorted to extend that same love and forgiveness to those who have offended us.

Three basic steps to forgiveness are:

1) Clearly define the offense to yourself.

2) If you have held anger, bitterness or resentment toward the offender, confess it to God.

3) Choose to release the offense (including your negative emotions and thoughts) to God.

If you have wounded each other through reluctance or refusal to forgive past hurts, now is the time to begin the restoring process of reconciliation. By sowing seeds of forgiveness, you will reap a harvest of unity and joy you may have forgotten was possible in your relationship.

KEY-TURNING APPLICATION

If you recognize areas of unforgiveness for past issues in your marriage, address them one at a time and walk through the steps to forgiveness. If you uncover some deep hurts within sensitive areas in the course of this exercise, we suggest that you invite a third party (pastor, Christian counselor, or mature Christian friend) to complete your discussion with you.

chapter ten

TRAPPING THE "LITTLE FOXES"

LADIES FIRST

Standing before the cross, you see your reflections surrounded by the crimson teardrops. You're appalled by your frown and petulant pouting lips. *Come on, honey, smile,* you tell yourself. *No one wants to look at that sourpuss.* You struggle to recompose your features, forcing your facial muscles to relax and smile, yet you cannot change their unattractive arrangement in the mirror.

Do I really look so selfish and bitter and angry? you wonder.

"Man looks at the outward appearance, but the LORD looks at the heart."

Where is that Voice coming from? Suddenly you feel embarrassed and exposed, as if you're in an important meeting and a blouse button has come undone or there's a piece of lettuce stuck in your front teeth.

"There is none righteous, no not one."

Something within you wants to argue with the Voice, to protest your honorable intentions in everything you do, but you know it's not true. Even in your best, most unselfish actions, you know you're still trying to make yourself look good in others' eyes. Either that, or you're trying to ease the pain of being yourself and never feeling worthy enough. You drop to your knees and bow your head.

"Come to Me, all you who are weary and heavy-laden."

Your eyes grow hot and wet with tears and you feel as if your entire head and torso are melting with relief. Yes, life *has* grown wearisome. No matter how much you try to serve others—your family, your friends, your church—you never feel as if you're doing enough. Life has lost its joy. There are no such things as "simple pleasures" anymore. It's all about striving and keeping up and meeting needs and pouring your efforts down a dark, bottomless hole. Where is that abundant life Jesus promised?

Now the tears flow. Not tears of sorrow or hurt, but of wonderful relief, as if you've just been snatched out of a canoe that was heading over Niagara Falls. You're caught up like Lois Lane in Superman's arms, only your Savior's identity is no secret. You know exactly who He is, and oh, it feels so good to be safe with Him.

"Confess your faults one to another."

You think of all the times you've inwardly criticized your husband or complained or made fun of him with your girlfriends. You've never actually cheated on him, but . . . *Oh, Lord, I've been so unfaithful to him in such sneaky little ways. How could I ever tell him? He'd never forgive me.*

Your husband turns to you and blurts, "Honey, I'm sorry for the way I ignored you yesterday while you were trying to tell me about Mr. Michaels. I know I was belittling you with my attitude. Actually, I was watching the game to put off balancing the checkbook. I'm so afraid of failing at providing for our family that every financial glitch throws me into a panic, and I end up taking it out on you. Can you find it in your heart to forgive me?"

"Your turn," says the Voice. "Now."

"Oh, honey, I've been so self-absorbed I haven't appreciated how hard you work for us. And I've had such a rotten attitude and made fun of you with my girlfriends. I know I was wrong to do that and I'm so sorry. Please forgive me."

"Of course I forgive you. Will you forgive me for being such a grump?"

Mr. Michaels smiles as the two of you embrace beneath the teardrop-framed cross.

"Mmmm, we should do this confession stuff more often. Have you seen a bedroom around here?" your husband whispers in your ear.

Sex is never far from his mind, but you don't want your host to overhear you. "Honey, shhh!" you say, giggling, with a glance toward Mr. Michaels. But the warmth generating from below your bellybutton has you wishing for a bit of privacy, too.

Clinging to each other, you rise to your feet, and the mirror reflects the love of Christ radiating back at you.

AND GENTLEMEN

Man, is that the picture of Dorian Gray or what? you wonder as you see your image in the cross-shaped mirror. You like to think of yourself as an okay-looking guy—maybe not in quite the shape you once were, but certainly no slouch. But this man in the mirror looks scared and insecure and much more calculating than you envision yourself. You pride yourself on your ability to make your friends laugh, but there's not a hint of humor in the face looking back at you from above your shoulders in the mirror.

Pull yourself together, man, you tell yourself, squaring your shoulders and pasting that pleasant expression on your face that you use when dealing with bank clerks and policemen.

"Man looks at the outward appearance, but the LORD looks at the heart."

Where is that Voice coming from?

Am I really such a cross between a scared little boy and a bully? you think. *Do I try to hide behind my image at work to appear self-assured and grown up?*

"There is none righteous, no not one."

Why is that Voice so unnerving?

"Aw, come on," you want to say. "Don't I serve on enough committees and coach enough of my children's sports? Don't I give enough money to charity and save enough kids from a life of crime on the streets by purchasing subscriptions to the magazines they're selling?" But you know that's not really what the Voice is talking about. You know all that stuff is just a futile attempt to build up an ego that's been trampled by never being quite tall enough, quite quick enough or agile enough or smart enough. You can't deny that you're trying to compensate for what you know is the underlying cause of so many problems in your life—pride. Too much pride to ask for help or to admit when you're wrong. Too much pride to go to God to ask for wisdom even when the panic rises in your chest because you don't know how to manage your own life, let alone the lives of your wife and children.

You drop to your knees and bow your head.

"Come to Me, all you who are weary and heavy-laden."

"Oh, God," you cry out inwardly. "I cannot do this. I want to be a good husband and father, but sometimes I just don't know how. It feels like nothing I do is ever enough and I'm always letting my family down."

"Confess your faults one to another."

Is it a fault to tune out when she's going on and on about stupid stuff that she really doesn't want my advice about anyway? And what's so wrong about snapping at her a bit when she's totally irritating me with her nagging about our finances?

Silence.

Conviction.

Okay, okay, Lord. You're right. I might as well get it over with.

You turn to your wife and blurt, "Honey, I'm sorry for the way I ignored you yesterday while you were trying to tell me about Mr. Michaels. I know I was belittling you with my attitude. Actually, I was watching the game to put off balancing the checkbook. I'm so afraid of failing at providing for our family that every financial glitch throws me into a panic, and I end up taking it out on you. Can you find it in your heart to forgive me?"

She looks at you, and her eyes are shining with tears.

"Oh, honey, I've been so self-absorbed I haven't appreciated how hard you work for us. And I've had such a rotten attitude and made fun of you with my girlfriends. I know I was wrong to do that and I'm so sorry. Please forgive me."

"Of course I forgive you. Will you forgive me for being such a grump?"

You pull her toward you, and she's all softness and sweetness and no resistance as you embrace beneath the teardrop-framed cross. You can't remember when you wanted her more.

"Mmmm, we should do this confession stuff more often. Have you seen a bedroom around here?

"Honey, shhh!" She giggles, glancing toward Mr. Michaels.

Clinging to each other, you rise to your feet, and the mirror reflects the love of Christ radiating back at you.

⋟✤⋞

Most of us have no lack of *present issues*, another gate in your Marital Mystery Tour. Like the "little foxes" of Song of Solomon 2:15, they do inestimable damage to the vineyard of your marriage. The little foxes are all the "lefts" in your relationship: the underwear left on the floor, the cap left off the toothpaste, the hair left in the sink, the ice cream bowl left on the counter, the shoes left in the middle of the living room, the thoughtless remark left hanging in the air. These countless minor grievances and irritations of everyday life leave your partner feeling left out of your heart.

When we were newly married, I had little tolerance for Alan's mistakes and did not want to be identified with them. If he made a wrong turn, misspelled a word or forgot the lyrics to a song, I would feel acute embarrassment. How could I (the "perfect" English major) be married to someone who would write "Your special!" instead of "You're special!" on a love note to me? Instead of being happy for his sweet thoughtfulness, I would fret over his ongoing misuse of "your" for "you're" (and "there" for "their" or "they're" and "it's" for "its" and so on).

I allowed his minor imperfections to overshadow the strength of character and maturity in Christ that initially had attracted me. Even today I want Alan to be always calm and unruffled. I have trouble accepting him when he expresses insecurity, fears, or anger. At those times I must make a conscious choice to allow Christ to be my strength, to focus on His perfection rather than Alan's lack thereof.

By the same token, Alan is irritated by my tendency to leave hangers on the bathroom doorknob, and he can't close the door without moving them. He wants dinner to be at a consistent time every night, and I lose track of time so dinner is consistently late. At certain times—like when we're eating dinner or watching a movie or sharing intimate time together—he doesn't want me to answer the phone, but I feel compelled to (just in case it's an emergency).

Alan has also had to learn to hear and accept my expressions of anxiety regarding finances (or childrearing or whatever weighs heavily on my heart) without trying to "fix" me. Did the following type of scenario ever occur in your home?

Alan (returning from work, looking around house, not smelling dinner cooking): Hi, hon. Looks like you had a rough day.

Pauly (sighing): Yes. The day just got away from me. The kids wouldn't take their naps, and all they did was fight all afternoon.

Alan (in a teaching tone): Well, honey, I've told you—all you have to do is discipline them properly and keep them separated. You just need to be more consistent, that's all.

At this point, many husbands seem to think their wife should gush, "Oh, thank you, honey! I didn't know that! You've really helped me." Take it from me, men. No matter what it sounds like to you, your wife is *not* asking for your advice in this situation. She is looking for acceptance and understanding and a listening ear. If she is anything like me, she has been "beating herself up" all afternoon for not being a "good" mother, not keeping the house tidy, not having dinner ready on time. What she needs is an arm around the shoulder and a little practical help with the children or with dinner or both. (By the way, when she wants your advice, she'll ask for it. It will sound something like this: "Honey, I could really use your help with this problem." Or "Do you have any suggestions of what I should do about this?")

Jesus came not to be served, but to serve. His Spirit lives inside you so you can do the same. When every fiber of your tired body cries out for rest, you need to cry out to Him for His love, His patience, His strength, and His grace to serve your spouse. By walking in the power of His Spirit, you can keep short accounts and encourage each other through the pressures of everyday life, thereby deepening your commitment to each other and strengthening your marriage.

KEY-TURNING QUESTIONS

1. What are three "little foxes" that keep you from appreciating each other?

2. Are you willing to let God change you?

3. Will you give your spouse freedom to address these areas when they arise?

    ❑Yes ❑No

    If yes, what and when are the best ways for these conversations to take place?

    If no, what must happen in order for that freedom to occur?

4. Discuss these issues now or set a specific time when you can discuss them later.

chapter eleven

CLOSING THE BACK DOORS

LADIES AND GENTLEMEN

Arm-in-arm, you stroll through the remainder of your vault tour.

"We must be deep inside the mountain," your spouse comments.

"You're absolutely right," Mr. Michaels agrees. "In fact, if we went any farther into this hillside, we'd surface on the opposite side. This very hallway, by the way, once led to another entrance, a back door, if you will. However, it opened out to someone else's property, and the rocky, steep terrain presented many dangers. Once, a man calling himself a 'soldier of fortune,' otherwise known as a thief, tried to break in that way and almost abducted the lady of the house. Afterwards, the owners permanently blocked off this exit."

"That's interesting," you say. "So there's no back door."

⋗✦⋖

Crisis situations, the final type of gate, arise in every life. Having vowed, " . . . in sickness and in health, in richer and in poorer, for better or for worse . . . ," you must expect those promises to be tested eventually.

At some point, you will face a job change or health problem. Alan and I have friends who have had to deal with such tragedies as the death of a child, catastrophic financial loss, and incarceration for white-collar crime. Some of you will have elderly parents move in with you. The husband of a woman I met suffered a head injury that left him with amnesia and altered his personality.

Our first great crisis occurred when Alan's left eye developed a swollen optic nerve during our second year of marriage. He underwent testing during a weeklong hospitalization that left the ophthalmologists and neurologists mystified. Their initial prognoses were grim—brain tumor or multiple sclerosis. But their battery of tests nullified those possibilities.

For six months, the doctors observed the progress of Alan's condition as his vision gradually deteriorated along with his patience and self-esteem. The doctors ordered him out of the gym, so he was unable to do gymnastics and questioned the validity of his ministry with Athletes in Action. At one point, the prescribed steroids, which caused emotional mood swings, incited such anger that he struck and broke our kitchen table with his fist.

"Who is this man?" I wondered.

Eventually, Alan's doctors recommended a visit to the Mayo Clinic. Then the Lord impressed Alan to approach the elders of our church requesting prayer, which he did. At his following weekly check-up, his ophthalmologist expressed surprise that his eye had stabilized. Gradually, the condition improved until his vision, which prior to the swelling had been 20-20, tested at 20-15 (practically bionic!)

As this mysterious affliction ran its course, our relationship ran through the wringer. My loyalty to Alan was tested as I questioned my ability to live with and love a man who, at times, bore little resemblance to the stable, enthusiastic Campus Crusader to whom I had made my vows. With Alan's emotional ups and downs, I was forced to rely on the Lord again and again as the source of my stability. Time after time Alan came to me asking forgiveness.

Together we were brought to our knees seeking the Lord's healing, direction and forgiveness as Alan's relationship with our gymnastic team's director ran through a course paralleling the deterioration and healing of his optic nerve. Ultimately, God used this trial to change the direction of Alan's ministry by taking him out of the role of athlete and into the position of administrator.

Like a couple of frontiersmen, Alan and I had hacked our way through a formidable tangle of emotional conflicts. The investment of physical and emotional energy we made in our marriage increased its value a thousandfold. Perhaps we saw things in each other we didn't want to see. Yet by committing ourselves to forge a path through the wilderness of anger and frustration, we were rewarded by a stronger relationship when we came out on the other side of the woods.

Years ago, Alan and I introduced a couple of our neighbors to a personal relationship with the Lord. Over the course of a year or so, we spent hours and hours of time with them. Both previously married, they were a handsome couple with two beautiful young children and a history of conflict in their marriage. As we talked through some of their issues, it became apparent that both of them saw divorce as an option "just in case" they couldn't resolve their differences. By leaving this "back door" open, they allowed themselves an escape route that should never have existed in their marriage. Eventually they divorced and moved away, leaving Alan and me with a sense of loss and futility and the knowledge that it didn't have to end that way.

As Christians we mustn't allow ourselves to leave open any back doors in our marriage. Knowing that God hates divorce, we must never threaten it in anger or even joke about it in fun. Our commitment to each other, like our Lord's commitment to us, must be unshakable.

KEY-TURNING QUESTIONS

LADIES AND GENTLEMEN

Relaxed and refreshed by a fragrant herbal drink concocted seemingly out of thin air by Mr. Michaels, you're enjoying the comfort and closeness of sitting side-by-side with your spouse on a loveseat tucked into a nook in the vault's wide hallway. Softly lit blue walls and fresh fragrant bouquets of roses and baby's breath create a garden atmosphere deep within the hillside vault.

"Down that hallway you'll find the precious gems, heirloom jewelry, gold and silver coins, and various savings certificates, stocks, and bonds belonging to your estate. Would you like to go inspect them now?" asks Mr. Michaels.

You both shake your heads. "Thanks, Mr. Michaels," you reply, "but that's not important to us right now. I think we've discovered the real treasure in the things we already have."

⤞✦⤝

1. Each of you recall a crisis you have endured together and describe how the experience has positively increased the value you place on your relationship.

2. Remembering that our commitment to each other is rooted in our commitment to the Lord, discuss the following questions with your spouse:
   a. Have I presented myself as a living sacrifice to the Lord?

   b. What are the areas in which you don't feel accepted by me?

c. On a scale of 1- to -10 (10 being the best), how would you rate your commitment level?

d. Using the information on forgiveness presented in this section, seek each other's forgiveness for past and present hurts inflicted on each other. Then pray together for greater commitment to each other.

SECTION THREE:
The Key of Communication

chapter twelve

WORKING FROM THE SAME PLAYBOOK

LADIES FIRST

"Allow me to show you the eyes and ears of your estate," Mr. Michaels suggests as you saunter arm-in-arm with your husband down a path away from the hillside vault. "See the satellite dishes and antennas on top of that hill?"

Your husband squints in the general direction indicated by Mr. Michaels' pointing finger.

"Honey, why don't you just put on your glasses?" you suggest. "You know you can't see a thing without them, so you just go around squinting. You're so silly. Nobody here cares what you look like."

Your husband stops walking and drops your arm. The romantic mood evaporates. *Poof*!

"What about you and your retainer, dear? You're just as bad. We paid all that money to get your teeth straightened; then you never wear the retainer to keep them that way."

Stunned by his angry response, you defend yourself. "The orthodontist said I only need to wear it at night, and I hate the way it looks, so I always put it in after I kiss you good night and turn out the light. Besides, what does that have to do with you and your glasses?"

But halfway through your retort, your spouse waves his hand in a brush-off gesture and walks away, catching up with Mr. Michaels after a few quick long strides.

You blush with embarrassment even though no one is looking at you and wonder what you did to set him off that way. *Golly, I was only trying to help him realize it was okay to wear his glasses if he couldn't see,* you tell yourself. *Isn't that what glasses are for anyway? And don't most Americans our age have some kind of vision problems? Why else would there be so many ads on TV for laser eye surgery and disposable contact lenses and buy-one-get-one-free deals on glasses?*

Alongside Mr. Michaels now, your spouse turns to him and—you're sure he's feigning interest—says pointedly, "As you were saying?" You can't see Mr. Michaels' face, but you just know he has raised his eyebrows as he slightly inclines his head and glances over his shoulder at you. Hot, angry tears sting your eyes, and you bite your lips, pretending to be intensely involved in looking for something in your purse. You exhale, close your eyes and tell yourself, *I'm not going to let this bother me.*

Lifting your chin, you courageously "put on a happy face" and trot over to Mr. Michaels' other side as he says, "The dishes and antennas make up part of a surveillance and communication system that coordinates all activities within these grounds. From the main office up there, you can see and hear what's happening in every room of every building, and talk with a supervisor at a variety of substations. Would you like to run up the hill and see the operation?"

At the word "run" your heart drops into your tired feet. Not only has the elation you felt just a few minutes earlier evaporated, but also gloom has gathered itself into a little gray cloud hovering just above your head. How can your husband look so composed and self-satisfied, as if nothing has happened, when exhaustion is threatening to overwhelm you? You resign yourself to trudging up the hill.

"How far is it?" you ask.

"Oh, about a half-mile." You wish you'd opted for hiking boots when you dressed this morning.

"But don't worry about walking up there," Mr. Michaels continues. "I parked an electric golf cart behind those bushes."

Yes! "Did you hear, honey?" you ask your husband. "We won't have to walk up that hill!"

"Huh?" he replies. "Could you repeat that? I wasn't listening."

AND GENTLEMEN

"Allow me to show you the eyes and ears of your estate," Mr. Michaels suggests as you and your sweetie stroll arm-in-arm down a path away from the hillside vault. There he goes again, interrupting your renewed musing about the location of the master bedroom suite. "See the satellite dish and antennas on top of that hill?"

You have to admit to yourself that the top of whatever hill Mr. Michaels is referring to looks quite fuzzy, but since you weren't driving, you've left your glasses at home. Those things are such a nuisance. Your vision was fine until recently, and you're not quite used to remembering to bring them along like a ladies' handbag everywhere you go. So you squint in the direction indicated by Mr. Michaels' pointing finger.

Then your wife says, "Honey, why don't you just put on your glasses? You know you can't see a thing without them, so you just go around squinting. You're so silly. Nobody here cares what you look like."

Who does she think she is—my mother? Why is she talking to me in that "teaching voice" of hers? Especially here in front of Michaels. Well, she's not so perfect herself. Your visceral response is a combination of annoyance, embarrassment and . . . what? Something from childhood, but you're certainly not going to analyze it here.

Shaking off her arm, you retort, "What about you and your retainer, dear? You're just as bad. We paid all that money to get your teeth straightened; then you never wear the retainer to keep them that way."

There! That'll show her she's got a few flaws of her own. But she comes back at you with more of that nah-nah-nah-nah-nah edge in her voice. "The orthodontist said I only need to wear it at night, and I hate the way it looks, so I always put it in after I kiss you good night and turn out the light. Besides, what does that have to do with you and your glasses?"

Oh, that tone of her voice never fails to drive you up a wall. She sounds just like your little sister tattling on you. You can feel pressure rising in your chest and head like steam inside your car's radiator, and you don't want your frustration to escalate into anger. You're tempted to make an obscene gesture, but, in that split second between thought and action, know you have to let go of your desire to retaliate. So feeling like a gangster dropping his weapon and surrendering to the police, you unclench your fists and quicken your pace to overtake Mr. Michaels.

What was he talking about before this little altercation? Something about antennas? And I was wondering about the master bedroom. Oh, yeah, then she made that stupid putdown about the glasses. Well, that sure cooled off the physical desire quickly.

You've got to release it and move on, so you turn toward Mr. Michaels and ask, "As you were saying?" It will be a welcome relief to talk to someone besides your wife for a while. Why does she have to make everything so petty and complicated?

Here she comes now, smiling at Mr. Michaels as if she doesn't have a care in the world. Of course not—she dumps them all over you.

Michaels continues his explanation: "The dishes and antennas make up part of a surveillance and communication system that coordinates all activities within these grounds. From the main office up there, you can see and hear what's happening in every room of every building, and talk with a supervisor at a variety of substations. Would you like to run up the hill and see the operation?"

Well, maybe now at last you'll be able to see the inner workings of this place and, perhaps, how Mr. Michaels does some of his little stunts, like that thing with your wife's bloody face. You wonder if the two of them planned that one in advance without your knowing about it.

That would explain it, but when would they have had the time to plot it out? Haven't you been together through the whole tour? What about when he first came to the door yesterday? Could they have conspired then? Who knows? Maybe she's been planning this thing for a long time, and Michaels' showing up at your door was just part of their scheme. It seems like quite an elaborate and expensive plot, but you're at a point where you don't really trust her. Now you begin to wonder how much this whole thing is going to cost you if she's charging it on a credit card.

Her nearly hysterical voice breaks into your thoughts. "Did you hear, honey?" she practically shouts at you. "We won't have to walk up that hill!"

You're caught totally off guard. "Huh?" you grunt. "Could you repeat that? I wasn't listening."

⚡

Three hard-of-hearing Englishmen converse on a bus in London. The first one asks, "I say, is this Wembley?"

"No," replies the second, "it's Thursday."

"So am I!" chimes in the third. "Let's all get off and have a drink!"

So it goes when we fail to connect with our partner in communication, only not with such humorous results. Early in our marriage, Alan and I could argue for an hour or more before realizing we were both saying the same thing!

Sometimes I, quick and articulate with my arguments, went for a win at all costs. Alan, in frustration, would slam the door as he walked out, leaving me mentally shouting my closing arguments at him.

On other occasions, fear of rejection would hold my tongue captive for weeks while I internally fretted about some offense Alan had unknowingly committed against me. As he puzzled about my emotional withdrawal, I struggled to find the magic words to release me from my silent prison. Finally, in an upheaval of "emotional vomit," I would spew out all my pent-up feelings. By this point, Alan would no longer recollect the incident, and I'd have to refresh his memory. Then we'd slosh around in the gooey mess for a while trying to locate the real issue amid the muck.

This ungodly pattern in our marriage changed in 1983 when we learned some communication skills from Dr. Dallas and Nancy Demmitt. The Demmitts' simple methods revolutionized the way we talk to each other, and we became certified seminar leaders a year later. Since then we've taught these skills to hundreds of people through our Communication Connections workshop.

Many couples fail to communicate simply because they never learned how. Alan and I want couples to quickly achieve some success and feel hopeful about their ability to discuss issues with each other. So during the course of the workshop, we present four specific communication skills and demonstrate how they work by discussing current issues from our lives—and our human fallibility becomes immediately apparent. Then we coach participants through various exercises implementing the skills.

We know that workshop participants profit from the amount of practice they get during our seminars. So as you and your spouse work your way through this section, we strongly encourage you to record yourselves as you complete each exercise. Then you can replicate a workshop atmosphere by hearing yourselves and reviewing how you communicate. Be sure to encourage each other with what you're doing right. (People usually realize their own mistakes as they listen to themselves, so keep your critiques of each other positive.)

Our *Communication Connections Workbook* presents a complete description of all four skills. But here we will focus on two major elements: *Talking Targets* and *Closing the Loop.*

How do you define communication? Some people might say that it's "getting my point across" or "saying what I mean as clearly as possible." True, precisely conveying your point of view is half the battle, but it's only your half. How do you know that your spouse has understood your perfectly articulated message?

Within the context of our workshop, Alan and I define communication as "the accurate exchange of information for understanding." When my partner can restate my message in his or her own words to my satisfaction, I am assured that I have been understood.

I've heard that football teams use something called a playbook. Having never played football myself, I have to trust Alan on this, and he assures me this is the case. All the players on a team use the same playbook, which describes who does what for each play, so they function as a unit when they take the field. Then when the quarterback calls a certain signal, all ten other players know what they're supposed to be doing to move the ball effectively toward the end zone.

I've previously mentioned Alan's and my differing family backgrounds. Consider how your and your spouse's varied upbringings affect your communication patterns. Our friends Margaret and Lee are prime examples of these differences. Margaret is a soft-spoken, southern belle whose family members rarely raised their voices at one another. Lee's family, on the other hand, fought World War III over every minor issue that arose around the dinner table. Margaret was appalled at the noise and emotion accompanying each meal. Yet to Lee this uproar was normal.

Do you men ever think you are brilliantly describing your position on an issue only to have your train of thought broken by a whimper? You look at your wife to see her curled into a fetal position, weeping. *What did I do now,* you wonder.

Or perhaps you ladies attempt to describe your hurt feelings to the back page of the newspaper while your husband buries his head in the sports section. His occasional grunts serve only to alienate you further.

We all need a "playbook" to unite our efforts when we attempt to resolve difficult issues. Our playbook consists of both skills and attitudes because *how we say what we say* is every bit as important as our words. A wife receives zero comfort and assurance when her frowning husband snaps, "Of course I love you—now leave me alone."

Additionally, you may fail to connect with your spouse because you don't have a common language to describe what's going on inside your skin. First you need to get in touch with yourself; then you need a way to help your partner conceptualize how you feel, what you think, what you want, and how you'd like to handle a particular situation. To help you achieve this type of understanding, our next chapter describes the *CommuniStar*, the first skill for your "playbook."

KEY-TURNING QUESTIONS

1. What do you see as the strong points and the weak points of your communication with your spouse?

2. What are the main issues that are most difficult for you to discuss as a couple?

3. If you could change one thing about the way you and your spouse communicate, what would it be?

chapter thirteen

THE COMMUNISTAR

LADIES FIRST

The electric golf cart hums along, traversing the steep hillside, but you can hardly enjoy the view. *Honestly, that man never hears a word I say*, you fret. *I might as well be talking to a corpse, for all the response I get from him. Now why did that have to happen, just when things between us were going so well?*

You try to analyze what went wrong. Why did he get so touchy about the glasses thing? You were just trying to help him see how silly it was to worry about how he looks in them—and you're sure it's a pride issue with him, a bit of vanity, like combing strands of hair over a balding spot.

"Pretty amazing place, huh?" You're startled by your husband's a-bit-too-cheery voice. "Who was it that we inherited it from? You never did give me all those details."

Just as you open your mouth to reply, "That's because I never *had* those details," another golf cart carrying a uniformed guard pulls alongside your cart. The guard touches his visor in salute to Mr. Michaels and nods toward you and your husband.

"Max, these are the new owners. We're on our way to COM Central," Mr. Michaels explains, driving on.

Max salutes again and speaks into his wireless earpiece, "Grounds patrol to Jerry. Michaels and two new owners heading your way."

Mr. Michaels parks the golf cart in a covered carport and leads you to the entrance, where he pulls a badge from his pocket and holds it in front of what you'd thought was a doorbell with a little red push button, but now realize is a type of scanning device. You hear two beeps, and the door glides open.

Gray industrial-grade carpet, granite walls and sparse furnishings create a no-nonsense atmosphere in the reception area. A guard stationed behind a podium greets you. "I've been expecting you, Mr. Michaels." He welcomes you and your spouse and hands you a badge similar to the one you saw Mr. Michaels use. "This badge will open all the doors to you in Communication Central," he explains.

"Thank you, Jerry. I'm taking them to the main station," Mr. Michaels says.

Jerry nods and pushes a button. As you walk away, you hear Jerry say, "Mr. Michaels and new owners approaching."

You examine your badge, intrigued by its gold-embossed emblem, a six-pointed star within a circle.

"Mr. Michaels, what is the significance of this star symbol?" you ask.

"That's the CommuniStar. It will give the two of you access to the mysteries of this estate so long as you choose to use it properly."

"There he goes talking about mysteries again. It makes me feel all tingly," you whisper to your husband. "I feel like I'm on the edge of some life-changing event, and I don't know what it is. How about you?"

After a pause he responds, nodding pensively. "Well, hon, I think it's all incredibly interesting."

You put your hands on your hips and stare at your husband, shaking your head. "Honestly, hon! I asked you how you *felt*, *not* what you *think*!"

AND GENTLEMEN

The uphill golf-cart ride gives you time to ponder how your wife and her buddy Michaels could have pulled off this huge, expensive hoax. You just can't figure out when she had the time or where she got the money to put the whole thing together. You haven't seen any unusual charges on your credit card bill, and she did seem genuinely surprised when Michaels showed up at your door. Maybe she's been taking acting lessons behind your back. *No, that's ridiculous*, you reprimand yourself. But you're sure she's in on the joke, or whatever it is. So you figure you'll just casually poke around and see if you can get her to admit to some prior knowledge, however inadvertently.

"Pretty amazing place, huh?" you begin. "Who was it that we inherited it from? You never did give me all those details." There— that sounded sufficiently innocuous.

But she's saved from answering by the arrival of another golf cart. The uniformed driver salutes Mr. Michaels, acknowledging you and your wife with a nod.

Where did they get all these bit-part players and their uniforms? They must have had to hire a whole cast of characters.

"Max, these are the new owners. We're on our way to COM Central," Mr. Michaels says.

Max relays the message with his Bluetooth device as your cart pulls away. "Grounds patrol to Jerry. Michaels and two new owners heading your way." *Good grief, where did these guys get their lines? From an old "Star Trek" episode?*

Leaving the cart in a carport, Michaels leads you toward an entrance, where a red light suggests a laser scanner. He holds out a card, and *Open Sesame!*

Another guard stands behind a podium in a stark foyer with all the charm of a cellblock. "I've been expecting you, Mr. Michaels." This guy is all business—you know immediately he'll never be your best friend, but you wouldn't mind having him on your side in a fight. He gives your wife a coded security passkey, saying, "This badge will open all the doors to you in Communication Central." *Why'd he give it to her instead of to me? One more indication of a conspiracy*, you conclude.

Michaels tells him he's taking you to a main station. As you walk away, you hear him acknowledge good ol' Jerry giving a heads-up to the rest of the crew.

Your wife examines the passkey as if it's a piece of heirloom jewelry. You have to admit you've never seen anything like the symbol embossed on it.

"Mr. Michaels, what is the significance of this star within a circle?" she asks.

"That's the CommuniStar. It will give the two of you access to the mysteries of this estate so long as you choose to use it properly."

"There he goes talking about mysteries again. It makes me feel all tingly," she whispers conspiratorially. "I feel like I'm on the edge of some life-changing event, and I don't know what it is. How about you?"

Is she for real? Or is this a set up? Now you *know* there are hidden cameras watching you. Better play your cards close to the chest.

You give what you think is a safe reply. "Well, hon, I think it's all incredibly interesting."

Hands on hips, she wags her head back and forth and glares at you. "Honestly, hon! I asked you how you *felt, not* what you *think!*"

⚜

My seventh grade home economics teacher organized the drawers in our perfect little "home ec" kitchens by outlining each utensil on white shelf paper. When I opened the drawer, I could see exactly where the spatula (or measuring spoons or potato peeler) belonged. Everything had its place.

In similar fashion, the *CommuniStar* helps you identify and organize each part of your experience of an issue. By defining what you think, how you feel, what you desire or expect to happen, and what you will do concerning an issue, the CommuniStar puts you in touch with yourself. Areas of marital conflict can sometimes re-semble volcanic islands surrounded by cloudy, shark-infested seas. If you can clear up the murky waters of your emotions, thoughts and intentions, you'll be better equipped to describe your position to your partner.

What constitutes an issue? When a particular discussion invari-ably leads to misunderstanding, hurt feelings, conflict or serious disruption of your relationship, it threatens the core of trust and intimacy that stabilizes your marriage. Such issues vary from couple to couple, but they often revolve around money, use of time, rela-tionships, sex, parenting and daily routines. Sometimes couples find it easier to avoid discussing these issues altogether, especially if one spouse tends to be a peacemaker. That way, they keep a superficial harmonious appearance when, in reality, any of those apparently dormant "volcanoes" could erupt without much forewarning.

Often when couples discuss negative, fairly "heavy" issues, their normal modes of talking together deteriorate into some form of manipulation. The CommuniStar and other communication skills Alan and I teach are best used to discuss these types of issues in your lives—we say, *more of the time for things that really matter.* Because these skills are structured and slow down the pace of your interaction, they're unwieldy for ordinary conversation. But that's precisely why they're so well suited for discussing the trouble spots in your marriage.

   * *Stop here and list three or four issues in your life. Remember an issue is a topic that causes or is a potential cause of conflict in your relationship.*

   (1)_____
   (2)_____
   (3)_____
   (4)_____

The CommuniStar

The CommuniStar works like a water filtration system to help you clear up the muck that surrounds potentially explosive issues in your interpersonal communication. It's a six-pointed star in which each triangle represents a piece of how you experience an issue.

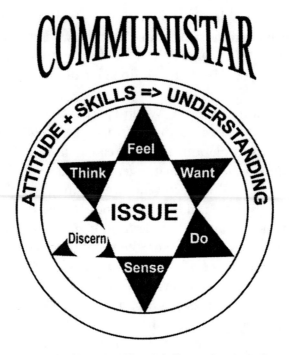

Remember: The goal is NOT to win, but to promote understanding.

Feelings

Beginning at the top of the star, the first point is labeled "Feel." How do I feel emotionally concerning this issue? Am I happy? Sad? Confused? Angry? Irritated? Elated? Annoyed? Upset? Women tend to be more aware of their emotions than men are, but men still have them. The CommuniStar helps you to pinpoint and take responsibility for those feelings (or to "own" them).

Thoughts

The first point to the left of "Feel" is "Think." What are my thoughts regarding this issue? How do I interpret what you did or said? Some "thought" words are "believe," "decide," "realize" or "feel that." Note that "feel *that*" is a lead-in to an opinion or thought; it's not the same as expressing an emotion using "feel."

In everyday speech, people often use "feel that" or "feel like" to express their thoughts or opinions. You might say, "I feel that the best course of action would be . . . " or "I feel like you're not really saying what you mean." These examples are expressing first, an opinion, and second, an interpretation. However, despite use of the word "feel," neither is relating an emotion. Be mindful of this fact, especially when your partner is asking how you feel (or felt) emotionally regarding an incident.

Intentions

The "Want" triangle defines our desires, expectations, or intentions. What is your motivation or desired outcome in this situation? What are you hoping will happen? Or in the case of a past instance, what were you expecting to happen?

This used to be a blind spot for me. In a feeble (and usually unsuccessful) attempt at unselfishness, I would ignore or deny my wants in a given situation. Returning from a party, for example, I might be silent and glum.

"What's going on?" Alan would ask with his annoying intuitive perceptiveness.

"Nothing," I'd mumble, staring out the window in misery.

After many "nothings" and "I don't knows," he'd finally hit upon the magic question: "What were you expecting to happen?"

Ah ha! The lights would come on, and I'd realize I *did* have expectations going into the party (or the meeting, etc.) Maybe I'd hoped for a quiet moment to talk with a friend, or for more intimacy or group interaction. Whatever they were, I wasn't in touch with my expectations enough to consciously realize that they weren't being met.

You, too, may possess similar blind spots in one or two of these areas. Using the CommuniStar will help you probe within yourself, bringing your thoughts, feelings or expectations to a conscious level.

You might also have intentions that are very clear to you but unrecognizable to your partner. For instance, desiring to demonstrate your concern that your spouse may make a poor impression on a potential client, you might say, "Is that what you're going to wear to your appointment?" Clearly (to yourself) you are trying to help improve your partner's chances for success. But your partner may feel threatened and accused, and could therefore respond, "Why are you always so critical of me?"

Here you are—the "good guy"—with every intention of helping your spouse, but your partner misinterprets your unstated intention and hears only criticism and negativity, making you the "bad guy."

Sensory Data

The bottom point of the CommuniStar, "Sense," represents your sensory data. On a physical level, what did you see, hear, taste, touch or smell that is affecting the way you view this issue? Did you see a certain expression on your partner's face that led you to believe he was upset? Do you hear an edge in his voice that you interpret as anger? Did the taste of the burnt toast irritate you? When you held her hand, did the palm feel sweaty, so you thought she was nervous? Did you smell roast beef cooking when you walked in the door and anticipate a delicious dinner?

The sensory data you perceive helps you to define and clarify the reasons for your interpretations of each other's actions. Simply reporting what you see and hear will help you objectify your partner's behavior and will minimize your tendency to blame or accuse. Compare, for example, the two statements below:

1. "You're mad."
2. "I hear your voice getting louder and see your fists clenched and your eyebrows knit together, and I think you're getting angry."

Or these two:

1. "You always let situations at work get you down."

2. "'I saw your shoulders hunched over when you walked in the door, and saw you drop your briefcase and sit down heavily in your chair with a long sigh, staring at the floor. And I thought, 'This is just like the last time he had a disagreement with his boss.'"

This technique helps defuse potential explosions before they occur by deleting the accusatory "you" that puts your partner on the defensive. We encourage you to be self-responsible, reporting your sensory data (what you see, hear, etc.) using "I" statements.

Be aware that using "we" instead of "I" may send a vague, under-responsible message. "We need to get the children to bed earlier" may be a true statement, but which of us is going to be responsible for seeing that it happens?

Discernment

The "Discern" triangle is reserved for spiritual or intuitive input. This area is the only one that may not be applicable in every situation, but its significance demands a spot in the CommuniStar.

Impressions received during prayer fall into this category. For example, "Honey, I've been praying about our old car and believe the Lord is leading me to donate it to the homeless shelter."

The Holy Spirit's conviction of sinful attitudes in your life also belongs in this point of the star. For instance, in a recent workshop, a man said to his wife, "I felt hurt when you gave me 'that look' yesterday when I asked you to pick up the mail on our way out the door."

After restating his message in her own words (more on this technique in the next chapter), she replied, "Both my hands were full, and I already felt like a packhorse. When you asked me to pick up the mail, I felt helpless and frustrated and used."

Sudden awareness of his insensitivity shot through him, and he took his wife's hand in his, looked her in the eyes, and responded, "I never even noticed you were carrying so much stuff!

I was so caught up in myself and what I wanted. The Lord just revealed to me how selfish I've been. I'm sorry for being so insensitive. Please forgive me."

That's discernment!

Actions

Finally we come to "Do," the action point—actions past, present, or future. What did I do, or am I doing, or will I do regarding this issue? Some examples:

Yesterday I went to the bank—*Past action.* (This helps to place the issue in context.)

I'm balancing the checkbook—*Present action.*

I'm going to make a deposit—*Future action.* (What you actually will do, not merely what you'd like to see happen. It's specific.)

Our "hot" issues often remain hot because we fail to conclude our discussions with satisfactory action points. I may understand how you feel and what you want, and you may know how I feel and what I want, but if we can't decide what we're going to do about it, we're laying the groundwork for future frustration. The issue remains unresolved.

You may be wondering why I didn't start at the top of the CommuniStar and proceed around it point by point. I deliberately hopped around the star because that's frequently how people process their issues. When we think of an issue, some of us may first be aware of what we saw or heard; others begin with an emotion; yet others, their own actions. There is no right or wrong way to perceive an experience—our perceptions are as varied and individual as our personalities. But to help your partner understand your point of view, you must eventually get in touch with all the points of your Star and then report them to your partner.

Contract

Perhaps an issue is too emotionally volatile or complex to resolve at one sitting. In that case, your action may be to recognize
that fact and choose to let it rest for a while. If you do, Alan and I
urge you to *contract* with your partner to discuss it later setting
certain parameters:

1. What is the issue? Be specific. It is best to discuss and resolve one at a time. Avoid "rabbit trails," that is, side issues
   that arise in the course of discussing the main issue.
2. Where is the best place to discuss it? In your bedroom? In a
   restaurant? Definitely not in front of the kids.
3. When will you discuss it? Set a date and time.
4. How long will it take? Fifteen minutes? Two hours? Plan
   an amount of time appropriate for the complexity of
   your issue.
5. How much energy will it take? Set a time when both of you
   can be alert and fully awake.

Most importantly, remember this is a formal agreement with
your partner. Keep the date as you would a business meeting or
other pressing appointment. In so doing, you will build trust into
your relationship with your spouse.

So how would you use the CommuniStar? Awhile back, our
family went on vacation, and I packed leotards and gym shorts so I
could work out while we were away. When I looked in our suitcase, however, my workout clothes were missing. (I had forgotten
that at the last minute I had given them to our son David as pad-
ding for his camera lens in his suitcase.)

My first (very human) reaction was to accuse Alan: "Alan, did
you take my leotards out of the suitcase?"

Alan's (very human) response was, "No, of course not. What
makes you think I'd do a thing like that?"

"Well, my stuff is missing, and I know I didn't take it out!"
(What a short memory I have! And so accurate!)

This little altercation could have escalated to nuclear war if Alan hadn't suggested we use the CommuniStar to discuss the issue—after going out to the car and finding my things in the trunk (where David had left them after he unwrapped his lens).

Alan: I *heard* you say (SENSE) your leotards were missing, and I *felt* (FEEL) very frustrated. I *thought* (THINK) you were unjustly accusing me, and I *wanted* (WANT) you to understand I didn't mess with your things. So I *went* out the car and *found* your stuff (DO), but I *would like it* if you wouldn't jump to conclusions and blame me so quickly (WANT).

Pauly: I *looked* (DO) in the suitcase and *saw* (SENSE) my leotards were missing, and I *felt* (FEEL) very confused and disappointed, because I *wanted* (WANT) to exercise, and I distinctly *remembered* (THINK) packing them. I totally *forgot* (THINK) giving them to David, and *I'm sorry* (DISCERN) I accused you of removing them. Please forgive me for blaming you.

As you can see, using the CommuniStar slows down the pace of the conversation. Remember, it doesn't matter what order you choose to report the elements of your star. As long as you touch each point, you give your partner a more complete picture of what is happening inside you. Can you see how opening this window to your soul will build intimacy in your marriage?

KEY APPLICATION

Choose one of the issues you listed earlier in this chapter. Using the two CommuniStar diagrams below, each of you map out your perspective of the issue. Being careful to remain self-responsible (using "I-statements"), describe your star to your partner.

If possible, record your conversation. When you play it back, listen for self-responsible "I's," blaming "you's," and under-responsible "we's."

chapter fourteen

DO YOU HEAR WHAT I SAY?

LADIES FIRST

At COM Central, you realize for the first time the size and complexity of your estate. Colored lights on a map the size of an IMAX movie screen denote the location of each security guard and checkpoint. Flickering screens—some segmented into halves or quadrants—reveal buildings, rooms and roads you had no idea existed on your property. Beyond the manor house, the hillside vault, and the tracts of land you've seen so far stretch facilities you know you won't be able to explore in this one day. A library, a fine arts museum, a sports and entertainment center, a business and industrial complex, a childcare center, elementary and high schools, an intimate chapel as well as a large church, and, of course, a shopping mall—Why, it could take a lifetime to learn all the ins and outs of these vast grounds!

"I can't believe all this is ours!" you exclaim to Mr. Michaels, feeling giddy with excitement and overwhelmed with a sense of responsibility. "There's so much here! How can we possibly own all this? Who takes care of it all?"

"You and your husband do," he replies, matter-of-factly.

"But how could that be? We just learned about it," you begin to protest.

At that moment, you feel a strange vibration in your right ear and, imagining a mosquito looking for a quick snack, you shake your head. You tap your ear with your fingertips then realize the insistent buzzing comes from the small cellular earphone Mr. Michaels clipped in place when you entered the building. Your heart begins to pound and you grab Mr. Michaels' arm.

"The phone is vibrating! What do I do?"

Mr. Michaels smiles, and your panic downgrades to apprehension. "Answer it," he replies.

"H-h-hello?"

"Hey, hon, it's me! These things really work! Aren't they cool?"

"Honey, you scared me to death!" You're relieved that it's not an estate official asking you to make a decision about the property, yet annoyed that your spouse is playing silly games during your tour. "Where are you? You should be here with Mr. Michaels and me learning about COM Central."

"I should, should I? Well, who told you to tell me what I should be doing? Your buddy, Michaels?"

"He's no more *my* buddy than yours, dear; he's our tour host."

"Right. So we're still playing that game, are we?" There's a pause, then, "Oh, sure, all right." Then, "Your pal Michaels says we should all meet in the COMStar Room."

"How could you be talking to Mr. Michaels? He's right here." But no, he's gone. *Wasn't I just holding onto his arm?* There he is, waving you toward a glass door emblazoned with the now-familiar CommuniStar logo. "Oh, no, never mind, I see him."

You hold your passkey in front of the red light and enter the COMStar Room, all the while insisting to your husband that you and Mr. Michaels are not deliberately deceiving him. *How can I convince him that this isn't a plot?* you ask yourself, watching for your mate's approach through the glass door. Although Mr. Michaels still stands with his back toward you on the other side of the door, somehow you hear his voice saying, "Use the Star. Use the Star."

The star? With sudden clarity you focus on the CommuniStar printed on the transparent glass. "Honey," you say, grateful for the tiny cell phone keeping you connected with your spouse, "I'd like to share my CommuniStar with you about Mr. Michaels."

"Oh sure, fine," he says, but you detect a note of sarcasm in his tone.

"I'm hearing you say, 'fine,' but I don't think you really mean it," you begin.

Now he raises his voice a bit. "If I *said* fine, I *meant* fine, dear." He speaks the word "dear" as if it's two drawn-out syllables—dee-ur. Now you know for sure that he *doesn't* mean fine, and you begin to feel stressed, your voice unconsciously tightening like a violin string as it takes on a whiny note.

You can see him now standing on the other side of the door with Mr. Michaels, the CommuniStar framing his face as you try to work your way around the points of the Star to get him to understand you. "Honey, I'm hearing you refer to Mr. Michaels as my 'buddy' and my 'pal,' and I think that you think he and I are plotting something. I feel sad and disappointed that you don't trust me, and I want to help you understand that I don't know any more about what is going on here than you do. Please come in here and discuss this with me."

"You know I can't get in there. You have the passkey," he growls.

You see Mr. Michaels tap him on the shoulder and whisper in his free ear. "What's he saying?" you ask.

"He says if I close the loop with you, the door will open automatically." You see him turn his face toward Mr. Michaels and hear him ask, "What's closing the loop?"

Mr. Michaels whispers something, and your spouse says, "He says I have to repeat back to you what you said, so here goes." His voice takes on a sarcastic, singsong pitch. "You really want me to know that you and Michaels aren't plotting anything. Right! Like I'm some kind of id—" He breaks off mid-word as Mr. Michaels taps him on the shoulder and whispers in his ear. You can see his neck and face flush, and he begins again in a more humble tone.

"I'm sorry, hon. Mr. Michaels informs me that he never saw or spoke to either one of us prior to yesterday. Can I try again?"

Finally, the lump in your chest begins dissolving. You can feel your shoulders relax and you realize how tense they were. "Sure, honey, go ahead."

"You want me to understand that you and Mr. Michaels have not been plotting anything behind my back, and you'd like to talk about it. And you're disappointed that I would think such a thing."

The tears start to run down your cheeks.

"Oh, yeah, and you're feeling sad."

Suddenly the door glides open, and you meet halfway across the room, embracing like lovers.

AND GENTLEMEN

COM Central is pretty amazing. The highest of the hi-tech gadgets you've ever seen—enough surveillance equipment to make the Pentagon look like Legoland. Every flat-screen monitor reveals another dimension of this estate you'd had no idea even existed. And a map that must be linked to a Global Positioning Satellite showing outposts, checkpoints, roads, tunnels, even flight paths far more complex than you'd thought possible for a single estate. *Who really owns this place? Can't be us. We're just ordinary people. Neither one of us ever had a relative this rich. And all that other stuff—banks, schools, stores, sports arenas—I'd have know if anything like that was ours.*

While your wife "oohs and ahs" with Michaels, you take advantage of the opportunity to slip away and poke around for yourself. Maybe you can locate a free computer terminal that will allow you access to learn more.

A ramp leads up to a second level giving you an overview of the area. You can see your smiling wife leaning toward your dark-suited host and feel a surge of jealousy. In spite of all Michaels' talk about this estate belonging to the two of you, you can't avoid seeing some resemblance to Robert Redford in that movie where he convinces

Demi Moore and her husband to let her sleep with him for one night in exchange for a million dollars. *Yeah, and what happened to their marriage? It was totally ruined.*

You feel a sudden urge to interrupt their cozy little twosome, in frustration clenching the hair at the back of your head in both fists and bumping the clip-on cellular phone Michaels gave you. Quite a little gizmo—they've progressed several generations of technology since the flip-phone you normally carry in your pocket. Suddenly your wife grabs Michaels' arm, and you frown with displeasure and suspicion.

Then you hear, "H-h-hello?"

Oh no! That thing must have automatically dialed her number when I bumped it. Well, I can't let her know it was an accident. "Hey, hon, it's me! These things really work! Aren't they cool?"

"Honey, you scared me to death!" *Right. I caught you a bit too friendly with Michaels.* "Where are you?" she goes on. "You should be here with Mr. Michaels and me learning about COM Central."

Huh! Who does she think she is? My conscience? "I should, should I? Well, who told you to tell me what I should be doing? Your buddy, Michaels?"

"He's no more my buddy than yours, dear; he's our tour host."

Oh boy, that grating teaching voice again. "Right. So we're still playing that game, are we?" A light tap on your left shoulder startles you and you practically give yourself whiplash turning toward it. *How did Michaels get here so fast? Wasn't he just down there all snuggly with your wife?* Now he's whispering in your free ear, "Let's all get together in the COMStar Room." Caught off-guard, you whisper back, "Oh, sure, all right," then say to your wife, "Your pal Michaels says we should all meet in the COMStar Room." *Whatever that is,* you add to yourself.

"How could you be talking to Mr. Michaels? He's right here."

How could he be in two places at once? you want to say. *He's here with me.* But actually, that's not quite true, either, because now you see him motioning her toward a door near the base of the ramp you took to the second level.

"Oh, no, never mind, I see him," she says, and with another jealous pang, you watch her cross the room toward him.

I'm gonna get her out of this place, you decide, starting down the ramp. *I'm gonna tell her I don't care how much money this place is worth, it's not worth losing our marriage if this guy Michaels is constantly coming between us.* And then you hear her voice again in your ear—you'd forgotten your cell phones were still connected. "Honey," she says, "I'd like to share my CommuniStar with you about Mr. Michaels."

Yeah? I'd like to whack him with mine. "Oh sure, fine," you say.

"I'm hearing you say, 'fine,' but I don't think you really mean it," she says.

Now you're getting irritated. "If I *said* fine, I *meant* fine, dear." Why can't she just accept what you say at face value? The next thing you know, she'll start her whining routine.

By now you've reached the door, guarded by old Michaels as if he's some medieval knight of the Round Table. You peer past him through the CommuniStar printed on the glass door, squinting to see your wife within. "Honey," she says in maddeningly high-pitched tones, "I'm hearing you refer to Mr. Michaels as my 'buddy' and my 'pal,' and I think that you think he and I are plotting something. I feel sad and disappointed that you don't trust me, and I want to help you understand that I don't know any more about what is going on here than you do. Please come in here and discuss this with me."

How can she know what I know? Well, I know what she does know. "You know I can't get in there. You have the passkey," you tell her.

There's another tap on your shoulder, and Mr. Michaels whispers in your free ear.

Immediately she wants to know what he's saying to you. *Can't a guy have a private conversation around here?*

"He says if I close the loop with you, the door will open automatically." You just want to get her off your back. But you have to ask Michaels, "What's closing the loop?"

He gives you his reply, and again she wants to be in on it. So you tell her, "He says I have to repeat back to you what you said, so here goes." *Oh man, I feel like I'm back in fifth grade. This is ridiculous.* "You really want me to know that you and Michaels aren't plotting anything. Right! Like I'm some kind of id—" There's that tap on your shoulder again, only much more insistent, firmer, bringing with it the thought that Mr. Michaels could dislocate your shoulder if he really wanted to. He whispers in your ear, "I was sent on assignment to you and your wife and met her for the first time yesterday at your door."

And an insistent, firm Voice inside your head adds, "Let he who is without sin cast the first stone."

You realize you've been condemning your wife based solely on conjecture. You feel yourself flush with shame and remorse for doubting her loyalty. Humbled, you start over. "Sorry, hon. Mr. Michaels informs me that he never saw or spoke to either one of us prior to yesterday. Can I try again?"

You're grateful for her gracious response. "Sure, honey, go ahead."

"You want me to understand that you and Mr. Michaels have not been plotting anything behind my back, and you'd like to talk about it. And you're disappointed that I would think such a thing." That was easier than you thought it would be.

Even without your glasses, you can tell she's crying—which reminds you, "Oh, yeah, and you're feeling sad."

The door opens, and you sprint across the room to hungrily pull her yielded body close to yours.

⸙

Have you ever tried to shop in a fabric store with three young children? Even normally obedient kids may be driven into mischief by the maddening power of sheer boredom in Cloth World.

Several years ago, when Josh, David, and Jessica were approximately nine, seven, and five years old, I decided to spare them and myself the torture of fifteen minutes in the fabric shop at the mall.

"You may go next door to the sporting goods store," I solemnly intoned, "but I want you all to stay together. If you get tired of looking at things in Oshman's, I still want you to wait for me there. Do not come looking for me back here. Stay there until I come for you."

"Okay, Mommy!" the kids all chorused as they turned to go.

Sudden inspiration prompted me to call them back. "Wait!"

Three pairs of innocent, questioning eyes focused on me.

"What are you going to do if you get bored in Oshman's?" I queried.

"Oh, we'll probably just play out there in the hall," answered Josh as the others nodded in affirmation.

Argghh! Immediately I envisioned the headlines: THREE SIBLINGS KIDNAPPED AT PARADISE VALLEY MALL!

"No, you won't," I declared. "I want you to stay in the store until I come for you. What do I want you to do?"

"Stay in the store until you come for us, Mommy," they chorused.

"That's right. Now you may go."

Whew! That took a little extra time, but it was worth it.

If effective communication involved only how dynamically I state my point, I could think of myself as a better communicator than I really am. But how do I verify that the listener is actually receiving the same message as the one I'm sending? Alan and I define communication as "the accurate exchange of information for understanding." Keeping that definition in mind, turn your attention for a few moments to how well you listen.

What types of things keep people—more specifically, you—from being good listeners? List a few here.

_____

_____

_____

_____

Our lives are full of distractions—noise from without and within. Televisions, telephones, computers, children, cell phones and iPods, not to mention our own physical, mental, and emotional exhaustion, preoccupation with work pressures, preconceived judgments, and negative attitudes all compete for our attention with someone trying to carry on a conversation with us.

Careful listening requires discipline—saying no to all those distractions to focus on our partner. By listening we send a message that tacitly states, "I care about you."

What are some ways you can let a person know you are listening to him or her? List them here.

_____

_____

_____

_____

The number one answer Alan and I get to this question is usually "eye contact." If I'm looking at you, rather than at the TV, computer screen, newspaper, or (in my case) laundry, you may be relatively sure you have my attention. As I set aside distractions (turn off the TV, CD player, radio, computer; put down the paper, book, contract, mail; send children out of the room; stop folding laundry), I set the stage for meaningful communication.

Be sensitive to your spouse's need to sometimes look up or down or away in order to gather thoughts. I'm personally uncomfortable with *Top Gun*-like "lock-on" eyes, where I feel caught in the crosshairs of someone's gun sight. Yet, overall, we need to maintain a reasonable amount of eye contact for maximum benefit in our communication.

How can you let your partner know you're listening attentively? You may lean slightly toward him or her with an interested facial expression. However, if that threatens your partner by "invading" his or her space, try leaning slightly back, maintaining a relaxed, open body position. Ask questions inviting further sharing (not grilling, correcting or changing the subject, and definitely not employing the intimidating "Why?"). Questions like, "Can you tell me more about that?" or "What did you do then?" demonstrate your interest to your spouse.

Maintaining some degree of physical closeness and/or touching is also helpful in most relationships. Alan and I joke about the "porcupine effect," my tendency to "stick out my quills" in the midst of conflict. Everything about my body language says, "Don't touch me," while what I want the most is his arm around my shoulder, or, if that seems too extreme, his hand on my knee or arm.

Initially, Alan didn't believe this tactic would work, fearing impalement on my "quills." But as I curled up in a fetal position at the opposite end of the couch, he scooted closer, stretched out a tentative hand toward my shoulder, and, lo and behold, the "quills" came down as I visibly relaxed my defenses. The amount of physical touch will vary from couple to couple, but we encourage you to try it—you might like it.

When Alan and I first learned these communication skills, we were challenged to ask each other the question, *What can I do to help you open up to me?* Or, stated differently, how can I set an atmosphere in which you feel valued and safe enough to share with me what is going on inside you?

I learned that Alan wanted me to stop folding laundry and look at him, even though I thought I was perfectly capable of listening to him at the same time—and besides, it was HIS underwear. Although my former roommate, Diane, and I were comfortable carrying on a discussion as we flitted from room to room doing housework ("Keep talking, Diane, I can hear you!"), Alan was offended that I would even attempt such a thing. He wanted full-face eye contact.

I, for my part, asked him to please allow me to finish my sentences and stop interrupting. And despite my quills, I wanted him to sit close to me and hold my hand, even when we were having a disagreement.

Take a few minutes now and ask each other the question, "What can I do to help you open up to me?" Record your answers below:

HE   SHE

_____   _____

_____   _____

_____   _____

_____   _____

_____   _____

"A gentle answer turns away wrath, but a harsh word stirs up anger" (Proverbs 15:1).

Have you noticed how often conflicts are triggered or escalated by how we say what we say, or our partner's interpretation of a tone of voice or gesture? The next skill will help you and your partner keep the lid on such emotionally tinged discussions. The diagram below illustrates the process we call *Closing the Loop*, which will assure you of the *accurate* part of your exchange of information. Be forewarned, this process will slow down the pace of your conversation. But which is better, to have one lengthy session that allows you both to be understood and may often result in conflict resolution, or to continue your communication patterns that often result in a broken relationship and emotional distancing for days and sometimes weeks or longer?

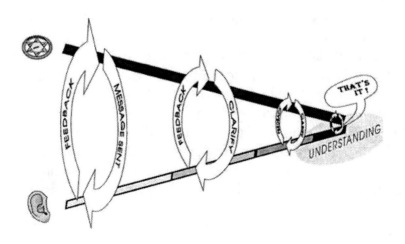

CLOSING THE LOOP
REFLECTING BACK THE IDEA YOU'VE RECEIVED

The small CommuniStar in the upper left corner of the diagram represents the partner who is sharing his or her Star, or the "sender." When an issue arises, the sender must first ask the other partner if he or she is willing to use the communication skills to discuss it. This simple question cues both of you to a need to change the pace of the discussion, to employ the CommuniStar and good listening skills, and to value each other's point of view enough to hear the other side of the issue.

The sender needs to present a clear, concise message using his or her CommuniStar. The receiver, depicted in the diagram by the picture of the ear, then "feeds back" the message to the sender. Rather than answering with an immediate response, the receiver, having listened for all parts of the Star, restates the sender's message in his or her own words.

Although the receiver is speaking, that does not mean he or she is now the sender. The original sender retains the floor and now has the opportunity to clarify his or her message. Perhaps the receiver missed an important point or skewed an attitude in a way not intended by the sender. This is the sender's chance to set the record straight.

These steps may be repeated any number of times until the sender is satisfied that the receiver has understood his or her message and affirms it, saying something like, "That's it!" or "That's right!" or, simply, "Yes."

Now the receiver becomes the sender, and the process repeats itself from the other partner's point of view.

Let's say Alan and I have had a spat over arriving late at church, and now Alan approaches me to discuss what went wrong. So he may say to me, "Pauly, I'd like to use our skills to discuss what happened yesterday as we were leaving for church." This introduction serves as a cue that I need to put down whatever I'm doing and choose to give him my full attention. At the same time, he's agreeing to play by the same rules, which, by the way, include valuing the other person even when we disagree about the issue.

After I agree, he'll continue, "I saw you fixing your hair and putting on your makeup at 8:30, and I felt concerned we were going to be late, so I asked you to please be ready to leave in five minutes. I needed to be on time because of some responsibilities during the service, and I thought if you were running late, you could drive separately. But I heard you say you'd be right with me. Then I saw you gather up an armload of laundry and head for the washing machine. I began to feel very frustrated, and I didn't want to yell at you, so I went out to sit in the car."

He may have more to say, but if I think this is all I can adequately handle, I may put up my hand (kind of like a traffic cop signaling "stop," but gently, of course) and feed back his message so far. "Alan, I'm understanding that you were feeling frustrated yesterday, because I was taking so long to get ready for church."

Whoops! *Notice I have neglected to give him his whole message.* If I had properly fed back his CommuniStar, I would have said something like, "Alan, I understand you saw me running late as I was getting ready for church and thought I could take the other car if I wanted to. You felt concerned because you needed to be on time. When you saw me take the clothes to the laundry room, you felt frustrated. So to avoid yelling at me, you went out to the car." It is now his turn to *clarify* his message, to help me understand the part or parts most important to him.

He says, "That's true; and I also said that if you were running late, you could have taken the other car, but I heard you say you would be with me right away, so I decided to wait for you. Then instead of coming right away, I saw you start doing laundry."

Notice he does not blame or make accusations, but he uses "I" statements to report what he saw me do and heard me say. This helps to keep me from becoming defensive.

My turn to feed back his message—I'm still not the sender. "So, your main point is I could have taken the other car, but you decided to wait for me because I said I'd be ready right away. Then I started doing laundry."

He agrees, "That's right."

151

At this point he may add to his message as long as he continues on the same subject, perhaps detailing further aspects of the issue and finally suggesting a possible solution. Notice that during the conversation thus far I've not defended myself or answered him with my point of view. That would defeat the purpose of the Closing the Loop process, which is to allow each partner the opportunity to be fully heard, valued and understood. Once Alan is satisfied that I've understood him, I become the sender and share my side of the issue until I believe that he has understood my viewpoint.

We may not have come to agreement, but both of us have been heard and understood. On more involved issues, we may each have to share and clarify and listen and feed back several more times. Sometimes just being understood is enough to satisfy the sender. On other occasions, one or both of us may need to repent of selfish attitudes before we can reach resolution. Understanding your partner's point of view is the first step toward resolving the issue. These skills alone won't solve the problem, but they can keep *how* you say what you say from intensifying the issue.

Regarding conflict resolution, remember Paul's admonition in Philippians 2:3: "Do nothing from selfishness or empty conceit, but with humility of mind, let each of you regard one another as more important than himself." He doesn't tell us to discount ourselves completely, but to balance our natural selfishness with the Lord's attitude of loving our neighbor as ourselves. And what better neighbor to start loving than your spouse?

KEY APPLICATION

Choose another issue from the list you developed in the previous chapter and use the Closing the Loop process to discuss it. Remember to preface your conversation by asking your partner to use the skills. Practice careful listening habits. Maintain physical contact, holding hands, touching knees, etc., if it helps you stay emotionally connected.

1. When you are the sender, remember to share your entire CommuniStar.
2. When you are the receiver, remember to stop your partner if you enter the "overload zone."
3. You may want to hold a small soft object, such as a Nerf ball or a feather, to signify who is the sender.
4. Record this exercise, if possible. Listen for I's, you's, and we's.
5. How do you rate your listening skills?
   - ❑ I know I have ears, but I've forgotten how to use them.
   - ❑ I'm hearing the words, but my judgments twist their meanings.
   - ❑ I let my partner go on for too long and get lost trying to remember the whole message.
   - ❑ This stuff is hard work!
   - ❑ That's it! These skills are terrific!

To receive more individualized instruction on communication and practice these communication skills in a small group setting, consider attending one of our Communication Connections Workshops. For more information, or to schedule a workshop in your area, visit our Web site: www.walkandtalk.org.

SECTION FOUR:
The Key of Completeness

chapter fifteen

GOD WANTS US TO ENJOY SEX

LADIES FIRST

Mr. Michaels clears his throat with a wisp of a cough. Your cheeks flush with embarrassment as you jump away from your spouse, smoothing your sweater. How long have you been kissing your husband, and where has his hand just been?

Unruffled as always, but with a slight smile warming his stalwart features, Mr. Michaels asks, "Would you lovebirds like to see Completeness Cottage?" Without awaiting a reply, he turns toward a concrete-block wall and appears to pass right through it. Beyond surprise by this point, you follow him, expecting at any moment to knock against a rough, solid surface. But like him, you and your spouse continue, unobstructed, beyond the wall, which dissolves into millions of tiny dancing particles as you move through it out to a cobblestone tree-lined driveway.

"Electromagnetic force field," Mr. Michaels explains. "It recognizes when you are in perfect harmony with God's plan for you, which is oneness with each other."

Your husband presses up against you from behind. "I could use more of that oneness," he whispers in your ear.

Again you blush. "Shh, he'll hear you," you whisper back. You have to admit to feeling a thrill of excitement at his amorous advances, but this is not the time or place for such expression, and you push him away.

"What does it take to get her in the mood?" he mutters.

The sudden clatter of hooves turns your head. A pure-white horse trots toward you pulling a gleaming white carriage with plush red velvet upholstery. Mr. Michaels, now wearing a topcoat and tall silk hat, effortlessly reins to a stop in front of you.

"What now?" groans your husband.

But you're enchanted. "Honey, isn't this romantic?" you exclaim.

"Uh, yeah, hon, it sure is," he says, as though reading from a script. A pause. You shoot a look at him, then at Mr. Michaels. You reach for the carriage, trying to decide how to get into the thing.

"Uh, let me help you up." Your spouse grabs you by the waist, lifts you onto a metal step, guides you into the carriage, then leaps in beside you. Pleasantly surprised by this show of gallantry, you look again from him to Mr. Michaels, whose full attention appears to be on the horse, which he now clucks into a trot. The jerk of the carriage on the bumpy cobblestones bounces you backward almost into your husband's lap. You both laugh and you snuggle contentedly in his arms until the carriage arrives ten minutes later in front of a vine-covered, thatched-roof cottage. Climbing roses ornament an arbor arched over a flagstone path leading to the front door.

Through a window you can see candlelight flickering softly within, lighting a four-poster bed dressed with a down comforter and mounds of pillows. Flames dance in a fireplace before a plush loveseat. A crystal decanter and two champagne flutes sit on a side table nearby.

"I think I've stepped into a Thomas Kinkade painting," you say with a sigh, planting a kiss on your husband's cheek. "Oh, honey, this is so romantic."

"So now are you in the mood?" he asks, winking and nudging you with his shoulder.

"Now don't go and spoil this moment by talking about sex," you say.

"Spoil the moment talking about sex?" he sputters, his voice cracking a bit. He sounds like an adolescent schoolboy, and you giggle.

"Don't laugh at me; I'm serious," he continues. "Weren't you just saying this is romantic?"

"Romantic, yes, but why do you always have to link romantic moments with sex?"

"Well, if romance isn't sexy, what is?"

Brain cramp.

You're spared from a very long and involved discussion by the appearance of Mr. Michaels next to the carriage offering you his hand. You step down onto the flagstone followed by your husband, who grabs your hand as soon as his feet touch the ground.

Like a sleight-of-hand magician, Mr. Michaels twirls his hands above his head and holds them out in front of you, an odd-shaped golden ornament dangling from each. "These two parts, so different from each other, combine to make one perfect whole—the key to your Completeness Cottage. Examine your part—it unlocks great mysteries for you alone."

It fits perfectly in the palm of your hand and you run your fingers over the rounded smoothness of one outside edge, puzzled by the jagged fractures, pits and ruts of the opposite side. It appears to be half of a heart shape, unevenly broken down the center, so flawlessly reflective you can see your face in it. Yet in its depths you see the face of your husband, first on your wedding day, then today; then words swim to the surface:

"How handsome you are, my beloved,
And so pleasant!
Indeed, our couch is luxuriant!"[1]

You choke back a sob as your heart fills with love and desire for this man whom God gave you, and you turn toward him to find him gazing at you with soft, wondering eyes. You reach for him,

---

[1] Song of Solomon 1:16.

and the ornament in your hand connects with the one in his. The resulting whole heart pulses and glows as though brought to life, the cottage door swings open, and hand-in-hand you enter.

AND GENTLEMEN

Oh man! It feels so good to be close to her again. *I've got to remember to use that CommuniStar more often*, you think. *I wonder if there's a large closet available—I know she'd like some privacy.*

Mr. Michaels' quiet cough ushers you back to reality and you realize your hands have been all over your wife's body. She jumps away from you straightening her clothing as if you were a couple of teenagers caught making out by her parents.

"Would you lovebirds like to see Completeness Cottage?" he asks, and you're sure he's gloating over the interruption of your embrace. *What is it with this guy? Doesn't he know I have needs? He sure seems to know everything else about me.*

The next thing you know he's walking right through a solid concrete wall. *How on earth does he manage to keep doing all this stuff?* But you follow him, braced to hit the wall. Suddenly you're on the other side, standing in daylight on a driveway resembling a "chick flick" movie set.

"Electromagnetic force field," Mr. Michaels is saying. "It recognizes when you are in perfect harmony with God's plan for you, which is oneness with each other."

Your thoughts have been far from the physical sciences. You're much more interested in a biological process at the moment and push yourself against the inviting roundness of your wife's backside. "I could use some more of that oneness," you whisper in her ear.

Obviously she's not in the mood. "Shh, he'll hear you," she shushes. Rebuffed, you drop your arms and mutter, "What does it take to get her in the mood?"

Clattering hoof beats. A flash of white horse followed by a flash of white carriage topped by Prince Charmingly Michaels himself.

"What now?" you groan. But she's been totally sucked in by this ridiculous fairy-tale display.

"Honey, isn't this romantic?" she exclaims.

You're about to throw up your hands in disgust and go look for a TV showing a football game—anything to take your mind off her voluptuous body—when Mr. Michaels' piercing look catches your eye. He nods his head, mouthing the word "yes."

"Uh, yeah, hon, it sure is," you say obediently, if mechanically.

Mr. Michaels' gaze continues boring into you as he tilts his chin toward your wife struggling to get a grip on that ridiculously anachronistic carriage. Slowly the light dawns and you grab her by the waist, mumbling, "Uh, let me help you up." You're surprised at how little effort it takes to help her onto a metal step and guide her into the carriage. Feeling pleasantly chivalrous, you bound in beside her. With a sudden jerk, the carriage starts forward, and your wife bounces backward almost into your lap. You laugh. *Well, Michaels, old chap, I guess you know a trick or two after all.* And you pull her close, nuzzling her neck and nibbling her ear and enjoying the fact that your tour guide has to keep his eyes on the road ahead of him. By the time he stops the horse in front of a way-too-flowery cottage, you've decided that carriage rides may be romantic, but they're much too bumpy for any serious kissing.

Through a window you can see a king-sized bed covered with all those ridiculous pillows women seem to like so much. *Aha! Now at last we're getting to the good part.*

Your wife gushes, "I think I've stepped into a Thomas Kinkade painting," and kisses you on the cheek. "Oh, honey, this is so romantic."

Finally! Just what you want to hear. "So now are you in the mood?" you ask, winking and nudging her with your shoulder, sure she'll get your drift.

"Now don't go and spoil this moment by talking about sex," she says.

You can't believe your ears! Isn't sex what this moment is all about? "Spoil the moment talking about sex?"

She giggles.

"Don't laugh at me; I'm serious," you continue. "Weren't you just saying this is romantic?"

"Romantic, yes, but why do you always have to link romantic moments with sex?"

"Well, if romance isn't sexy, what is?"

She appears stumped by your question, to which you'd very much like to know the answer.

But once again Mr. Michaels comes to her rescue, offering his hand to help her out of the carriage. Your jealousy sparks. *Hey, Prince Charming, don't get too chummy; she's mine!* You clamber out after her and grab her hand.

Mr. Michaels' eyes crinkle at the corners with a smile meant just for you. Then he waves his hands above his head like David Copperfield and extends them toward you and your wife. *What does he have there—Christmas ornaments?*

"These two parts, so different from each other, combine to make one perfect whole—the key to your Completeness Cottage," he says. "Examine your part—it unlocks great mysteries for you alone."

You stare at the golden object he drops into your palm, squinting at the ragged edge of its half-heart shape. How could something made of pure gold crack like that? Or was it designed that way, requiring a counterpart to be made whole?

Despite your missing glasses, you can clearly see your reflection—then, beyond it, your wife as she appeared on your wedding day; then, as she looks at this moment poring over her own piece of the heart. Words appear, words of a song you've seen in your Bible but never applied to her:

"How beautiful you are, my darling,
How beautiful you are!
Your eyes are like doves."[2]

Your heart fills with such pure love for your wife, your entire being aches with the wonder of it. You gaze at her as though seeing her beauty for the first time. Then she reaches for you, and the

---

[2] Song of Solomon 4:1.

half-heart you hold connects with hers. The resulting whole pulses and glows as though brought to life, the cottage door swings open, and hand-in-hand you enter.

⚜

GENESIS 2, REVISITED

"Adam, it's not good for you to be alone, and none of these animals is a suitable partner for you. Can't you see? They don't have your spiritual nature. Not one of them walks and talks with Me the way you do. That's why you're so lonely and feeling unfulfilled."

" . . . not good for you to be alone . . . not good . . . alone . . ."

The words seem to hang suspended in the air above his sleep-laden head as Adam's eyes flicker open and shut again. What happened? Why is he lying here in the garden in the middle of the day?

The last thing he remembers is his midday walk with the Lord God. Creating names for the animals had been challenging and fun until gradually he realized they were all coming to him in pairs. Observing their romping and mating dances had stirred something within him—a restlessness whose source he could not name, a craving for something he had never seen.

In an effort to rouse himself, he rubs his eyes and stretches his arms out to both sides. "Oomph," he grunts, "what did I do to my ribcage?"

"Adam! Are you awake?"

"Getting there, Lord," he replies groggily to the Voice behind him. "Wow, was that a deep sleep!"

"Well, turn around, Adam, and look here. I have someone I'd like you to meet."

Someone? Adam's eyes pop open. He bolts upright and whips around to see this someone.

"WOW! This is it! Yes!"

⚜

Imagine Adam's glee upon discovering the "helpmate suitable for him" designed by his Father and presented to him by the Lord God. She's the one whose body goes in where his goes out, whose softness complements his hardness, whose spirit unites with his in communion with their Maker. Imagine their perfect innocence and abandonment in lovemaking, their freedom of expression, their absolute trust in each other.

Now imagine God's pleasure in their union. Isn't this truly a wonderful thing He has done, designing these two to reflect His own spiritual essence and the love He Himself has for them?

Surely our Heavenly Father delighted in Adam and Eve's sexuality. Hear Him bless them, "Be fruitful and multiply, and fill the Earth, and subdue it." In other words, "Enjoy each other, children! And have lots of babies. This whole planet is yours."

Yet Adam and Eve disobeyed, and their perfect union was instantly marred. Shame, guilt, and death entered their universe. They went from walking with God in the garden to hiding from His all-knowing eye, dodging His questions in futile attempts to justify themselves. They tried to cover their once innocently naked bodies with fig leaves, and then watched in horrified remorse as their Lord killed two animals for their hides. They had never seen anything die.

God simultaneously pronounced both judgment and redemption. Paradise was lost forever to them. Previously joyful, Adam's work became hard and unfruitful. Eve was promised pain in childbirth and disharmony in her marriage. And their curse extended to every person who would follow after them.

A terrible disaster, yet all was not lost. God also promised salvation beginning with the words, "Your seed will bruise his (Satan's) seed on the head." This foretold Messiah eventually arrived on Earth to cleanse His people from their sin and return them to a state of grace, wholeness, and unity with Himself.

Prior to the fall, God planned for one man and one woman to be married for life, a covenant relationship reflective of His love for the worldwide community of believers. This plan has never changed. Jesus reiterated His Genesis mandate when He said in Matthew 19:5, "For this cause a man shall leave father and mother and cling to his wife, and the two shall become one flesh."

Adam and Eve's relationship with each other originated in the perfect, unbroken spiritual relationship they maintained with God. Their physical nakedness reflected their total openness with God and each other. Because they had no sin, neither had they anything to hide from each other—no guilt, no shame, no manipulative behaviors.

But the fall changed all that—separating them not only from their Lord, but also from each other. Instantly they blamed each other and shaded the truth in their communication.

In Christ, marriage relationships have been restored. But we have to do our part to maintain them, just as we service our vehicles or any other piece of equipment we want to operate smoothly. We must ask God daily for power to maintain oneness and openness. And as often as we ask in faith, God gives it.

Many couples struggle with their sexual relationship because they seek physical intimacy without establishing intimacy in two other vital areas of their lives: the spirit and the soul. God intended marriage to be a three-way union—God at the head of the relationship and a husband and wife mutually submitted to Him.

STOP AND THINK

Do you agree that marriage is a three-way union between a couple and God? Why or why not?

_____

_____

_____

_____

SPIRITUAL INTIMACY

We must not underestimate the importance of our relationship with God and how it affects our spouse. In the "vine and branches" passage of John 15, Jesus tells His disciples, "Apart from Me you can do nothing." This "nothing" includes marriage. True intimacy in marriage is impossible apart from both people selflessly giving to each other in the power of God's Spirit.

Does it seem odd to you that your willingness to give unselfishly to your spouse should be connected to your personal devotional life? How else are you to find the unselfish energy to keep on giving when you're mentally, physically, and emotionally drained, or simply don't feel like it? The Almighty God who loved you enough to give His only Son as a sacrifice for your sins continues to give to you and through you today—if you will let Him.

In Ephesians 5:18, Paul exhorts believers to be filled with the Spirit. When Alan and I heard Corrie Ten Boom, beloved author of *The Hiding Place*, speak at Wheaton College in the 1970s, she illustrated this point. Holding up a glove, she asked, "How much is this glove able to do?" The obvious answer: nothing. As she pushed her hand into the glove, Corrie asked, "Now how much can the glove do?" Filled with Corrie's hand, it could do whatever Corrie wanted it to do.

Like that glove, we are powerless, empty shells until the "hand" of the Holy Spirit reaches into our lives to move us according to God's plan. And, like two gloved hands clasped in prayer or grasping a tool, marriage partners may work together in unity for His purposes, including their sexual fulfillment.

We need to learn to "breathe" spiritually, keeping short accounts with the Lord. Described in Campus Crusade for Christ's popular "Four Spiritual Laws" booklet, spiritual breathing entails (1) confession of sin, or "exhaling" and (2) asking for the Holy Spirit's infilling, or "inhaling." This practice, made possible by faith, is introduced in I John 1:19 ("When we confess our sins, He is faithful and righteous to forgive us our sins and to cleanse us of all unrighteousness") and Ephesians 5:18 ("...be filled with the Spirit.")

When my faith in God was new, I understood that I was forgiven for my sin, but I didn't know how to deal with recurring sinful attitudes and actions in my life. A little doubt here, a little anger there—here a "'tude," there a "'tude." Suddenly I seemed more full of sin than I'd been before I asked the Lord into my life.

My naturally melancholy personality led me to painful hours of self-examination and false guilt until I learned to breathe spiritually. God's Word directed me to confess my sin, rather than drag myself through torturous self-flagellation. Once a sin is confessed, He promises to forgive and cleanse me. Then, like Corrie's glove, I am ready for His Spirit's "hand" to fill and move me however He desires.

As you "breathe" spiritually, you are less prone to riding a roller coaster of spiritual highs and lows through stretches of broken fellowship with God. Your walk with God acquires a stabilizing constancy that, in turn, permeates your personal relationships, including your marriage.

Apart from a vital relationship with God, you lack resources to draw upon. Your "well" of love, joy, peace, patience, kindness, goodness, faithfulness, gentleness, and self-control (the fruit of the Spirit) quickly runs dry unless you remain continually filled with God's presence.

STOP AND THINK

How can spiritual breathing help your sexual relationship with each other?

_____

_____

_____

_____

INTIMACY BETWEEN SOULS

Webster's New World Dictionary of the English Language defines *soul* as " . . . the immortal or spiritual part of the person and, though having no physical or material reality, is credited with the functions of thinking and willing, and hence determining all behavior." The soul has three parts: the mind (which thinks), the emotions (which feel) and the will (which chooses). In a healthy marriage, partners connect in all three areas.

The Mind

Our *mind* is our major "sex organ." I have often climbed into bed thinking of my "to do" list knowing Alan had a different "to do" in his mind. Sometimes I've been stewing over some hurtful remark he shot my way earlier in the day (long forgotten by him). Too busy or too miffed to express my thoughts to him before going to bed, I've sat next to him, absently (though suggestively) rubbing his back and legs, chatting in stream of consciousness about my day (turning him alternately on and off). If I'm serious about my sexual union with him, I must discipline my mind to focus on his pleasure, and he on mine.

I know I'm not the only one needing a mental overhaul in this arena. If intellectual delinquency weren't a universal problem, Paul would have had no need to instruct us in Romans 12:2 to "be transformed by the renewing of your mind." The problem, as he explains in verse 3, is that we think more highly of ourselves than we ought to think. In other words, our thoughts revolve around ourselves—our hurts, our opinions, our selfish desires, and so on and on and on.

STOP AND THINK

On a scale of 1-to-5, how *selfish* or *selfless* are you within your sexual relationship?

How I View Myself	How My Mate Views Me
selfish 1 2 3 4 5 *selfless*	*selfish* 1 2 3 4 5 *selfless*

How I View My Mate	How My Mate Views Him- or Herself
selfish 1 2 3 4 5 *selfless*	*selfish* 1 2 3 4 5 *selfless*

What are you willing to do to improve this?

_____

_____

_____

_____

You must discipline your thought life in order to connect mind-to-mind. "Taking every thought captive" and judging your thoughts according to a godly standard, you must ask yourself some probing questions:

Does this thought honor God?

Am I committing mental "murder" by criticizing one of God's beloved ones (including myself)?

Am I dwelling too long on a negative factor in my marriage?

Am I replaying a past incident or interchange with my spouse, allowing irritation to build into anger or self-pity?

Take a moment to consider the above questions and write down your response.

_____

_____

_____

_____

The Will

Even casual thoughts are serious business with God. Sometimes they act as an almost imperceptible backdrop to your life. You may carry on with normal tasks and conversations, but underneath a placid surface, a potential whirlpool threatens to swallow your unity.

When you become consciously aware of your negative thoughts, you're faced with a choice—to hold on or to let go. Letting go is as easy as spiritual breathing—confession ("Lord, forgive me for this wrong thought") and filling ("Lord, please fill me with Your Spirit and Your thoughts.")

Sometimes you need to verbalize what you've been thinking, feeling, wanting. (Use your CommuniStar.) At times you may think your mate should somehow (perhaps by osmosis) know what you think and feel. In the bedroom this assumption can have disastrous consequences.

Sometimes, earlier in our marriage, as Alan and I prepared for bed, he'd be hoping for sex, but he'd think, "Boy, am I tired. I hope she will initiate this process." Meanwhile, I—equally tired and having sleep as my goal—would be thinking, "What is he doing? He says he wants physical intimacy tonight, but he just rolled over. What am I supposed to do now?" I didn't even want sex, and I'd feel resentful and manipulated into getting things going.

At such times, our *wills* determine if we can work out a mutually satisfactory arrangement. Although we may both be "out of gas" from our day, one of us must decide, "I am willing to initiate this process and serve my spouse, not because I feel like it at the moment, but because I know that she/he will enjoy it." Or, "Maybe I need to forego my desires tonight and wait until tomorrow."

In Philippians 2:5-8, the apostle Paul describes how Jesus made selfless choices. He humbled Himself to the point of a humiliating and painful death. We need to do the same. Fortunately, in our case this death is not physical—it may be death to our way of doing things, or to our pride. It may be realizing and admitting to our spouse that our behavior or words have been hurtful.

At times I'd rather die physically than admit to Alan that I've been wrong. I've experienced sweaty palms, dry mouth, churning stomach, gritted teeth, and chewed cuticles attempting to avoid confessing my sinful thoughts, words, or attitudes to Alan. Desperate to end the conflict, I'd take the blame for the whole thing, saying something like, "I'm sorry, honey. It was all my fault. I shouldn't have . . . Please forgive me." Once I'd taken the blame for our squabble, Alan would be glad to be off the hook.

That is, until we hit an impasse about ten years into our marriage. A trusted and wise friend helped me understand that whatever the issue was, the conflict wasn't entirely my fault. I needed to take responsibility for and confess only *my part* of the sin involved in our conflict and trust the Lord to bring Alan to recognition of his part. I could then (by faith) forgive Alan and move on in freedom from bitterness.

The Emotions

Lastly, the soul contains our *emotions*. Patrick M. Morley, in his insightful devotional book for couples, *Two Part Harmony*, says, "Emotional love includes nonsexual touching—hugs, kisses, pats, squeezes and holding hands. . . . How do we achieve this? Frankly if we will simply treat each other like we would treat a stranger! Think of the attention, common courtesies, and interest we show perfect strangers."

Our emotions affect our sex life positively and negatively. Because emotions fluctuate based on circumstances, hormonal balance, and other physical factors such as energy or blood-sugar levels, they are not reliable gauges of our true state of being. We must be careful not to allow emotions alone to govern our physical relationship.

A popular slogan of my hippy days was, "If it feels good, do it." Crosby, Stills, Nash, and Young extolled the joys of "free love" with the lyric, "If you can't be with the one you love, love the one you're with." Throwing off the shackles of legalism, free thinkers promoted a philosophy that said when something *feels* right it must *be* right.

As Christians we understand that right and wrong are based on the Truth of God's Word, not our feelings. We may try to pray and get discouraged because we feel distant from God and question if He even hears our prayers. Yet the Bible says, "Ask, and it shall be given to you; seek, and you shall find; knock, and it shall be opened to you" (Matthew 7:7) and "Let us therefore draw near with confidence to the throne of grace, that we may receive mercy and may find grace to help in time of need" (Hebrews 4:16).

When your feelings conflict with the Truth of the Word, which are you going to trust? You must learn to act according to the unchanging Truth of Scripture no matter how you feel.

Although premenstrual hormonal buildup is no laughing matter for most women, the glut of PMS jokes making the Internet rounds testifies to the pervasiveness of this problem. I know what it's like to wake up in the morning feeling all the physical sensations—nervous stomach, pounding head, flashes of adrenalin—that usually accompany anger for me. For years I responded to these sensations as if I actually were angry and practically "bit the heads off" anyone in my family with the nerve to cross my path during those days.

The point is that our emotions can and often do lie to us. Yet we shouldn't disregard them totally. We must find within us the balance between rational truth and emotion. I have friends who cry so easily they're embarrassed and apologize for their tears. I, on the other hand, wish I could cry more often, but the tears don't come.

My emotional friends get whipped around by their highs and lows like riders on a carnival Tilt-A-Whirl. They feel as if they're either in ecstasy or on the brink of disaster. Others who are more like me tend to rationalize or deny emotions. They may not recognize what their emotions tell them. Or they stuff them so far down inside, they don't even know the feelings are there. But they're there, all right—and they surface eventually in tones of voice, or passive-aggressive behaviors, or procrastination, or outbursts of anger.

Marital love requires a balance between feeling and doing. In the honeymoon phase, couples are physically drawn together by the magnetic passion of young love. But familiarity, unresolved conflict, physical exhaustion, and numerous other eroding factors wear away that initial ardor, and wives find themselves saying, "I don't feel like it tonight, honey," or "I'm too tired," or the proverbial, "I have a headache."

Truthful as these excuses may be, the Word of God says in 1 Corinthians 7:3-5 to satisfy each other's sexual needs. This is for your protection and overall well-being. Yet to enjoy maximum sexual satisfaction, you must first connect soul-to-soul.

You may need to override your initial emotion by a choice of your will and ask yourself, "What is God's desire in this situation? What is best for my spouse right now?"

Sometimes pushing through your reluctance to engage in sexual intimacy results in not only a physical release but also an emotional one. I'll feel closer to Alan for having given up my "right of refusal." I'm not encouraging total denial of feelings, but they need to be weighed against God's mandate for marriages, "and the two shall become one flesh."[3]

Yes, God wants us to enjoy sex. But the best, the most intimate sex results from connecting first in the spirit and the soul.

---

[3] Genesis 2:24.

KEY-TURNING QUESTIONS

1. Discuss how your emotions affect your intimacy with your spouse. In what ways do your feelings enhance or block your ability to relate closely to one another?

2. Identify a time your emotions have misled you and share the incident with your spouse.

chapter sixteen

CAN MEN HAVE NEEDS?

LADIES FIRST

The interior of the cottage lives up to its promise from the outside, delighting and soothing your senses. Fresh floral arrangements adorn the coffee table and dresser. Candles and firelight illumine the sitting area and bedroom with a soft, inviting glow. Piped through built-in speakers, your favorite love songs float in the air. Someone has even drawn a bubble bath at just the right temperature in the large, oval tub, and two fluffy terrycloth robes hang on hooks within arm's reach of it.

You sigh, becoming aware of how tired your feet are from the day's explorations, and all you can think of is how good that bath will feel. You kick off your shoes with every intention of sliding into the tub.

But your honey has other intentions. "Hey," he says, pulling you toward him. "The bath can wait. Look at this bed."

Now you feel torn. A nap would feel really good, but you know he's not directing your attention toward the bed so you can sleep. You feel another sigh coming on, a sort of semi-agitated, semi-disgusted, totally selfish expression of your suppressed emotions. But then—even though he discreetly stayed outside when you came in—you hear Mr. Michaels' voice in your ear. "Look at him. Honor him. Respect him. His needs are every bit as legitimate as yours."

You gasp in embarrassment, wondering how much your host can see through the windows and whether or not your husband heard his voice just now. But your husband has already closed the curtains and locked the door—he knows how important privacy is to you.

As he begins removing pillows from the bed, you know you must choose. Do you give in to your "fate," as though succumbing to an unpleasant inevitability? Or do you joyfully participate in celebrating your husband's manhood?

Pondering these questions, you start to pull your sweater over your head, then feel your husband's arms wrap around your bare midriff. "Hey, sexy, not so fast. Let me help you with that."

Considering the last few pounds you've gained, you feel more self-conscious than sexy. But you stifle a denial rising to your lips when you hear another whisper in your ear, "He's telling you the truth. Let him love you. Respond to him."

Something melts inside you, and as your sweater drops to the floor, your arms drop around your husband's neck and all you can think of is how good it will feel to lie next to him naked in that king-sized bed.

AND GENTLEMEN

Frou-Frou, you think, glancing around the sitting room and adjacent bedroom within the cottage . . . but nice. You lock the door behind you, thinking, *I know she really likes her privacy, and the last thing we need is Mr. Michaels bouncing in here with 50 more fun things to do on our estate tour.* With that thought in mind, you close the curtains. You don't need any "peeping Michaelses," either.

Hey, get a load of that bed. Now somebody was thinking of me and my priorities when they put a king-sized bed in here. Romantic music to put her in the mood, even a big tub to soak in after we share in some "afternoon delight." Hearing your wife sigh, you realize she's showing a little too much interest in that bathtub.

Your heart starts to sink. You've felt jerked around like a yo-yo all day and now that you've finally got a few moments of privacy with her, the sexual tension that's been building up inside is demanding release. You can't decide whether to yell at her like a bully or whine like a hurt little boy. But you hear Mr. Michaels whisper in your ear, "Neither. Be gentle. Let her know your need." You've stopped wondering how he gets inside your thoughts and decide to simply respond as gently and lovingly as possible.

You know she's worn out, too. But maybe, just maybe, she'll have it in her to give you a little bit more. "Hey," you say, pulling her toward you. "The bath can wait. Look at this bed."

You can see she's struggling with her decision, but all you can do is hope she'll find it in her heart to give herself to you. Your loins ache with desire, but you're a man, not a boy, and you know you can exercise self-control if you must. Still, one can always hope for the best, and you begin removing pillows from the bed, praying she'll see it as more than a place to take a nap.

In the mirror over the dresser, you catch her reflection as she stands in the bathroom doorway, crossing her arms in front of herself the way women do before they grab the bottom of a sweater and pull it over their head. The exposure of her soft flesh heightens your desire, and you drop the last pillow, leap across the room and wrap your hands around her ribcage. You hope your voice sounds casually inviting as you say, "Hey, sexy, not so fast. Let me help you with that."

You feel the tension go out of her body; her sweater drops to the floor, her arms drop around your neck and you want to shout with Adam, "WOW! This is it! Yes!"

⋙◆⋘

Alan and I don't pretend to be experts in the field of sexual intimacy. When we were first married, Christian bookstores offered little practical, "nitty-gritty" advice regarding the sexual side of marriage, or what Dr. Tim LaHaye and his wife and co-author, Beverly, call *The Act of Marriage*. With my promiscuous background and resultant guilt, I grappled with my own desires—that seemed to get turned on at odd hours of the day when Alan wasn't around to satisfy them—and a difficulty expressing to Alan how he could tap into those desires when he had "the urge" and I didn't—which seemed to be much of the time. In my experience, doing what came naturally didn't work all that well.

At first, I got very little sleep. I'm a light sleeper anyway, and Alan would frequently roll over in bed, nuzzling and bumping me from behind. I'm certain he was delighted to have someone to nuzzle and bump, but he kept waking me up, and I would wonder if he "wanted sex" (which he probably did, but didn't need a half-dozen times a night). After a couple of sleepless weeks, I ended up one evening with a temperature of 103 degrees, took some aspirin, and got the first solid night's sleep of our marriage. But we both held hope in the words of our older and wiser friends Gloria and Robert Purnell, who, 25 years into their marriage, told us, "It just keeps getting better."

A year later, we heard an audiotape called "Sexual Technique in Marriage" by the late Dr. Ed Wheat, whose practical tips gave us a language with which to express ourselves more accurately and freely in this area. Just hearing Dr. Wheat say the words "clitoris," "penis," and "orgasm" without any apology or embarrassment emboldened me to express more of my needs to Alan.

But the quest for mutual sexual satisfaction was a long way from over. We've now spent 32 years experimenting, arguing, repenting, apologizing, discussing, forgiving, practicing, discussing some more and practicing some more. Until here, now, at last, are the Hellers' "Top Twenty Tips for Make-your-mate-smile Sex":

1. Psychologist Dr. Kevin Leman says, "Sex begins in the kitchen." We need to work all day at keeping mystery and romance alive in our marriage. If you men don't recognize

the value of your wife when she's up to her ears in diapers and dirty dishes, she'll probably be less than responsive to your amorous advances at bedtime.

2. A woman wants a whole relationship, not just sex. The 1995 novel and movie *The Bridges of Madison County* depicted a woman who sees herself as plain and unappreciated until a stranger uncovers her creativity, intellect, and femininity, and she awakens to become that wholly alive beauty in a brief affair with him that she secretly treasures for the rest of her life. Be advised, men: You, too, have the power to either bring out this latent beauty or to squelch it (as her husband did) in your wife.

3. Women yearn for romance for its own sake, not as a means to an end. You men can't expect that if you bring home flowers, light a few candles, or run a bubble bath that your wife will immediately want to have passionate sex with you. Maybe she wants to just enjoy the quiet candlelit moment with you and talk about her day and hear about yours. Ask her what she considers to be romantic, and then incorporate those things into your relationship.

4. Women want nonsexual touching. They like to be held and stroked and cuddled without feeling obligated to give anything in return. Otherwise they may end up feeling like sexual objects, mere receptacles for their husband's sperm. Sorry to be so blunt, guys, but that's the way your wife feels if you don't demonstrate that you value her for her other qualities and contributions to your marriage.

5. Keep short accounts, that is, be quick to ask forgiveness for any hurts and misunderstandings to maintain emotional oneness.

6. Be sensitive to each other's needs—physical as well as emotional. A husband's testosterone-driven need for sex is every bit as viable as a wife's need to cry or vent her feelings during an estrogen-charged, hormonally challenging day.

7. Husbands, recognize when your wife is overloaded and offer to help without waiting to be asked. If you happen to see the crying baby tugging on Mommy's pant leg while she is trying to help Junior with his math and little Sissie with her spelling, and the dirty dinner dishes are still piled in the sink, I hope you're not also thinking, "I wonder if she'll be up for a little action tonight." Sometimes washing the dishes and putting the baby to bed are the sexiest things you can do.

8. Understand that criticism and anger kill emotional oneness. Weigh your words and be aware of subtle (or not-so-subtle) underlying messages in your tone of voice and facial expressions.

9. Wives, we really have no choice in this matter—we're commanded to R-E-S-P-E-C-T our husbands. Stop what you're doing right now and take a deep breath, close your eyes, and thank the Lord for giving you this man to be your lover, hero, provider, and protector of your home. Think of all his positive attributes and plan ways to let him know how much you appreciate him for these things.

10. Wives, remember that when you're having sex with your husband, you're meeting his number one need. Don't treat it lightly. You're making a connection with him that can't be made in any other way. You're intensifying the magnetic attraction that keeps him coming back for more and prevents his eye from roving elsewhere to get that need met.

11. Sex provides both of you with a release of tension, physically and emotionally, while providing you with a way to be sensitive to each other as you learn how to make sacrifices, and to give and receive pleasure.

12. Keep some practical aids nearby: personal lubricant, Kleenex or a washcloth, breath mints or gum, lotion or massaging oils for backrubs or foot rubs, romantic music, candles and matches.

13. Be aware of your personal hygiene. In this case, cleanliness IS next to godliness.

14. Most women need privacy. Does your bedroom door lock? Are the children occupied so they won't distract you? Some of our friends used to "swap for sex" and take turns babysitting for one another's children to ensure uninterrupted time for intimacy.
15. Agree not to answer the phone. Let your voice mail or answering machine do it for you.
16. Do things to keep some of the mystery alive, like turning the lights down low and slow dancing with all your clothes on just to feel your bodies moving together. Feed each other strawberries dipped in chocolate, then lick the chocolate off each other's fingers—whatever serves as more of a prelude to sex than just taking of your clothes and getting into bed.
17. Take advantage of the resources available to you: books, CDs and tapes, DVDs and videotapes. Focus on the Family (Dr. James Dobson), FamilyLife (Dennis Rainey), *Marriage Partnership* magazine, the Association of Marriage and Family Ministries (AMFM—Eric and Jennifer Garcia), Real Relationships (Drs. Les and Leslie Parrot), Smalley Relationship Center (Drs. Gary and Greg Smalley), and the National Association of Marriage Enhancement (NAME—Leo and Molly Godzich), not to mention our own Walk & Talk Ministries (www.walkandtalk.org) are just a few who provide expert marital advice via conferences, the Internet and bookstores.
18. Realize that not every experience has to be a perfect "10," that is, your ideal of mutually explosive, simultaneous orgasms. Sometimes a woman is willing to settle for a "quickie" to please her man and move on to the next thing in her busy life. But be sure to have a meaningful connection, when you're focused on each other's pleasure, at least once a week.
19. Make dates for these special sessions of mutual pleasuring, especially if you know your spouse has a "prime time."
20. Be willing to talk about your preferences with each other. Does your spouse like foot rubs or back rubs or neck rubs? Tickles or back scratches? A variety of positions?

Looking into each other's eyes? These things are best discussed in a relaxed setting when you have plenty of time and no interruptions.

Which brings us to our final tip-top tip: Set aside a few days once or twice a year to get away with each other—AND WITHOUT THE KIDS—to focus on your relationship. Alan and I call these getaways "Triple-R Weekends" for Romance, Recreation, and Renewal. If you think you can't afford to pay for weekend—or midweek—getaways, consider the following: During the course of our marriage, Alan and I have stayed at friends' cabins and vacation homes, retreat centers, timeshare condominiums (freebies with a 45-minute sales-pitch), inexpensive motels, and more luxurious resort hotels (during off-season). We've been amazed at how God has provided for us to enjoy these times together. I think He's glad we're doing it and delights in helping us along. We've even had several friends who volunteered to baby sit for *all three* of our (high-energy, sweet-to-rambunctious) kids since we lived hundreds of miles away from our family members.

Even before Alan and I were married, Athletes in Action encouraged us to schedule bi-annual personal retreats to spend time with the Lord assessing objectives and praying about future plans and dreams. Back then, I wasn't even sure what an objective was. Alan is the goal-oriented one in our marriage. So he had to be the prime mover in our goal-setting department, and I basically "went along for the ride."

I don't know if others are as planning-challenged as I was; I think my chromosomal "map" totally missed the exit for the goal-setting gene. But as we discussed and wrote down our desires for the future and I gradually saw them become reality, I began to value the process for the focus it gives to my life. Through the input of mentors over the years, we started organizing our objectives in seven areas of our life and keeping track of them in notebooks.

Here are the seven areas:

1. *Spiritual*: your personal relationship with God; prayer, Bible study, devotional life.

2. *Marital*: using the five keys of Comradeship, Commitment, Communication, Completeness, and Consecration; planning to attend seminars, retreats, Bible studies, or fellowship groups to build into your relationship.
3. *Physical*: taking care of your body in the way God designed it to be kept; diet, exercise, weight control, health issues.
4. *Financial/Vocational*: budgeting your income to stay debt-free; providing for your family's needs; charitable giving.
5. *Parental*: rearing your children according to godly principles to guide them into mature God-honoring adulthood.
6. *Psychological/Intellectual*: how you think and process information; continuing education; stewarding your mind by maintaining an eternal perspective on today's circumstances.
7. *Social/Ministry*: your relationships with others in your church, your neighborhood, your work setting, and the world.

During our planning sessions, Alan and I each take some time alone to write out personal goals for these areas. For instance, in the physical area, I might write:

1. Maintain weight and cardiovascular health by exercising at the gym three times a week.
2. Walk the dog for a half-hour every afternoon.
3. Take all vitamins and medications in my regimen daily.
4. Get to bed before 10 P.M. every night in order to wake up early enough to get to the gym before work.

After this individual time, we review our goals with each other. Many of them may require cooperation; for instance, enforcing children's bedtimes or determining effective means of discipline, or creating and sticking to a budget, and so on. Your particular areas of prime concern will reflect your and your family's changing needs. Alan and I used to spend hours discussing our children's discipline, development, and educational needs, but those days have passed for us. Now we discuss how to best spend our empty-nest years and maximize the wisdom and experience we've gained.

Here's where you need to utilize teamwork and avoid finger pointing. We recommend starting these sessions with prayer. Discussing life-shaping issues raises the possibility of potential conflict, so use your CommuniStar and listening skills and avoid judgmental attitudes and defensiveness. Your very real spiritual enemy would rather get you to argue with each other or avoid talking about potentially divisive issues than see you face your issues head-on and make headway in resolving them. After all, the fruit of resolved conflict is oneness, while avoidance leads only to greater distance between the two of you.

Organizationally challenged as I am, I used to write notes to myself on slips of paper that I'd invariably lose. I've since learned to use a Palm Pilot to keep track of my life, while Alan prefers a notebook that holds his calendar, address book, and other papers. Whatever method you prefer, bring it with you on your Triple-R Weekend to "put shoe leather" to your goals. As you decide on specific steps you plan to take to meet your goals, mark them on your calendars so they remain a reality after you return home. Close these sessions with prayer, asking God's blessing and further direction as you live out the plans you've made. All of this adds up to the *Renewal* in our Triple-R Weekend.

Lest you think all we do on our getaways is sit around and plan, I remind you of the other two R's, *Romance* and *Recreation*.

Alan is a golfer, and I've learned to swing a club and connect with the ball enough to keep it moving in the general direction of the flag on the green. More often than not, our recreation includes a round of golf. I see it as a long amusement park attraction that includes bouncing around in a cart, hitting a ball with a club, looking for the ball, and cheering for each other's good shots.

I have decided to participate in the intense pleasure Alan receives from playing this game, and it has become my joy to do so. For his part, Alan has learned to "stop and smell the sales" in gift shops and bead shops and yarn shops and touristy clothing stores. We've poked around in musty museums and antique stores. We've strolled the manicured grounds of Victoria, B.C.'s Butchart Gardens and taken high tea at the Empress Hotel. And even though he's not a bona fide coffee drinker, Alan indulges my passion for tall decaf two-pump mochas whenever possible. We both enjoy hiking on trails that don't raise too much of a sweat, sliding down water slides that don't create too much of a "wedgie," and screaming on roller coasters that don't make us throw up at the end of the ride.

In other words, we've developed lots of ways to have fun together, and that's what the *Recreation* "R" of the Triple-R Weekend is all about.

For "instant romance," we pack candles and CDs of mood music. And we set aside plenty of time for enjoying each other's company between the sheets.

Finally, men, remember that romance is not found merely in the things that you do. A wife may say, "It's romantic if you show up unexpectedly at the office and take me to lunch," or, "It's romantic if you send me flowers (or bring me flowers)." But there's more to a romantic gesture than just the action, and that's the attitude behind it. It's the idea that you want to lavish upon your wife an unexpected gift that you know will please her and will build a feeling of intimacy. It expresses the idea, "You are really special to me and I've been thinking about you while we've been apart." Doing those special things is effective, not because your wife has said, "This is what I want," but because you're demonstrating that you want her to feel special in your eyes.

But we women also need to remember to applaud the efforts of our guys because it doesn't take much to discourage them in their romantic efforts. Here's what Alan has to say about it: "A man's wife will finally tell him what to do to be romantic. And then he'll do it and she'll reject him because she had to tell him what to do and she is suspicious since it's only been a week since she told him and now he's doing the very thing she asked him to do. *How romantic is that if he didn't think of it himself,* she thinks. Yet at first, the process of learning anything new requires following someone's instructions, and is mechanical at best. Then gradually, hopefully, it will become second nature to your husband. Or he can find a way to make it seem spontaneous, even if it's asking an administrative assistant to mark on his calendar three romantic things to do for his wife in the next six months."

KEY-TURNING QUESTIONS

1. Discuss what each of you thinks would be a romantic date.

2. Look at a calendar and determine a time that you can take your own Triple-R Weekend during the coming year. Talk about where you would like to go and what you would like to do during that time. Dream big and pray about it.

3. Rate your sex life on a scale of 1 to 10. Discuss what you and your partner can do to help improve it in the areas of knowledge, technique, emotional closeness, or romance.

4. Discuss what stage of life you are in and how it affects your sexual life (for example, exhaustion from taking care of babies and toddlers, empty nest, etc.)

5. Determine if your issues require the aid of a professional counselor or clergy member. Do not be ashamed to seek help—most couples need it at some point in their marriage.

SECTION FIVE:
The Key of Consecration

chapter seventeen

HOLY MATRIMONY

LADIES FIRST

You hear Mr. Michaels' now familiar *tap-tap-tap* on the cottage's front door just as you finish re-applying your lipstick. Perfect timing!

In the snuggly afterglow of your lovemaking, you'd almost forgotten your host was waiting outside. But then your husband had brushed the hair off your face, kissed you on the forehead, and tenderly whispered, "That was terrific—you totally satisfy my needs. But now I'm starved. Let's go see if we can find something to eat around here." You'd smiled, kissed him on the tip of his nose, and headed for the bathroom.

You slip the lipstick back into your purse, about to hurry to answer the door remembering how your day had begun with your host's knock and your frantic dash out to his limousine. But your husband touches your elbow and says, "Hey, no need to rush, hon. I'm ready, too. Let's go together." He reaches the door in a couple of long strides, pulls it open, and with a flourish, makes a gallant

Musketeerlike bow. "After you, m'lady." You grin, pretending to gather up a long, full skirt and sweep past him through the doorway, but he catches you by the waist and waltzes you out the door.

Outside Mr. Michaels awaits you, still formal, yet his eyes sparkle with the look of a proud grandparent watching his grandchildren at play.

You stop in your tracks and stare at him. He's standing on what looks like a cloud hovering about six inches off the ground. He reaches out a hand to help you step up, and your husband joins you without a word.

You're riding on a cloud!

Without any apparent effort or movement on Mr. Michaels' part, the cloud glides past the buildings, gardens, hills, and meadows of your estate. Sometimes it barely skims the ground; then it soars high over wooded mountaintops. With your arm around your husband's waist and his encircling your shoulders, it never even enters your mind to be afraid. You simply exist, happy to share each glorious moment of the ride with him.

The cloud lands and dissipates. You're standing in front of a one-room building that appears to be fashioned from chiseled glass or ice or perhaps a gemstone. Whatever it is, it glows in the lowering sun's nearly horizontal rays. Within, a linen-covered table set with a gold wine goblet and a matching platter holding pieces of matzoh, the unleavened bread used to celebrate the Jewish Passover, occupies the center of the room. A simple kneeling bench is the only other furniture.

"This is Consecration Chapel," Mr. Michaels says.

You don't see a door. "How are we supposed to . . .," you begin. But Mr. Michaels puts a finger to his lips and hands your husband a palm-sized white book with gold letters that shoot out brilliant multicolored rays of light. If you almost shut your eyes, you can read the bright letters through your eyelashes: "Holy Holy Holy."

You reach out to touch the book, but Mr. Michaels says sternly, "No, your husband is the priest of your home. He must carry this responsibility for your marriage. Let him lead the way."

A small, but authoritative Voice within you says, "This is right." You nod and look expectantly at your husband. He, too, nods as though he's been having his own conversation with Mr. Michaels, and walks with you toward the chapel.

"Mr. Michaels says that as I wash you in the water of the Word, I'm sanctifying and loving you," he says. "So here goes." He opens the book and reads, "John 14:6: 'Jesus said to him, "I am the way, and the truth, and the life; no one comes to the Father, but through Me." ' "

Without moving, you and your husband are inside the chapel. Holding your hand, your husband leads you to the bench, and you both kneel. He breaks off a piece of unleavened bread and blesses it. You open your mouth and he places the bread on your tongue.

He picks up the goblet and holds it aloft in blessing. Through the chapel's clear ceiling, you can see the stars coming out. You feel your heart swell with emotion that has nowhere to go but through your tear ducts. The tears spill out and stream down your face.

"Thank You, Lord, for this wonderful, safe, intimate place You have provided for me in this man, in this marriage. He is all the husband I've ever wanted and all I ever shall want for my life," you say. And you take the cup your husband hands you and drink deeply.

AND GENTLEMEN

When you hear Mr. Michaels' *tap-tap-tap* on the door, you're glad you gave your wife plenty of notice to get herself up and ready. That was some of the most satisfying sex you've had in a long time, but now you're feeling hungry. *I wonder if Mr. Michaels has a pizza with him.* You smile at the thought of your dignified host wielding a pizza box and standing outside by a pickup truck with a magnetic pizza sign attached to the roof.

But the sight that greets you when you dance your wife out the door drives all thoughts of pizza from your mind. *Is that honestly a cloud he's standing on?* By this time, you've ceased looking for gimmickry in his doings. This is a genuine cloud. It has no motor, no steering mechanism, not even a floor. Yet when Mr. Michaels helps your wife up onto it, she doesn't fall through. You step in beside her, amazed to be standing firmly on nothing. What can you say? This guy's the real deal.

The cloud travels smoothly through the air, apparently directed solely by Mr. Michaels' will. With an arm around your wife's shoulders, you decide to enjoy the moment with her. Seeing the grounds of your bountiful estate in all their grandeur fills you with awe. *Why did I not know sooner that all this was mine*, you wonder. *Especially this terrific woman. I've really taken her for granted.* And you hold her close.

You land in front of a one-room transparent building glowing in the setting sun's golden light. You've always liked the quality of light at this time of day, regarding with pleasure the halo-effect playing in your wife's hair.

"This is Consecration Chapel," Mr. Michaels says, and you realize the nature of this building. You feel a sudden urge to take off your shoes as if you're tracking mud onto brand-new carpet. You realize Mr. Michaels is watching you. He's smiling. His lips don't move, but you hear him say, "Yes, this is holy ground. And not only this building; your entire estate is holy, consecrated, set apart for just the two of you, and to fulfill God's purposes for you."

He sets a white leather book on the palm of your hand. Bright flashes of multicolored light inscribe "Holy Holy Holy" on the cover. Though you see Mr. Michaels converse with your wife, you hear his voice tell you, "You are the priest of your home. You sanctify your wife by washing her with the Word of God. You provide the spiritual covering your wife and family need. You each have your own personal relationship with God; but as far as your marriage is concerned, you are the leader. This is *your* responsibility, not hers. You lead the way."

You know this is right. You nod yes.

With the holy book in one hand and your wife's hand in the other, you walk toward the chapel, but see it doesn't have a door. What to do? "Read from the book," says Mr. Michaels' voice inside your head. "It's the key to Consecration Chapel."

"Mr. Michaels says that as I wash you in the water of the Word, I'm sanctifying and loving you," you tell your wife. "So here goes." The book falls open and you read, "John 14:6: 'I am the way, and the truth, and the life; no one comes to the Father, but through Me.'"

The wall that was in front of you is now behind you, and you recognize both the setting and what you must do. Taking your wife's hand, you draw her toward a low, cloth-covered table set for communion. Together you kneel on the bench by the table, and you pick up a piece of matzoh from the gold plate. The words "Lo, this is the bread of affliction" run through your mind along with images of a slaughtered lamb tied to a large stone table and a bleeding, naked man hanging on a roughhewn cross.

In heartfelt response, you call out, "Thank You, Heavenly Father, for sending Your Son, the promised Messiah, Jesus, to die in our place. We are so grateful." And you break off a piece of the brittle unleavened bread, and place it in your wife's mouth, before partaking of what remains.

You look into the blood-red wine filling the gold goblet. "Take and drink; this is My blood." But it's not Mr. Michaels' voice you hear. It's the Voice of infinite Love incarnate. You don't know how you know this, but you do.

With clasped hands, you raise the goblet upward along with your heart, your devotion, your destiny. The sky outside is darkening, but you feel your soul filling with light. Yes, this is right. You are priest of your home and protector of this woman by your side. You swear you will never allow anything to come between you. She belongs to you, you belong to her, and you both belong to God.

You drink from the cup and hand it to your wife.

⚜

Growing up in Jewish homes, Alan and I celebrated Passover with our families every year. In keeping with tradition, my mother had a set of Passover dishes, an entire collection of dinnerware that she stored in the basement and used only during the eight-day Passover celebration. To eat off the Passover plates at any other time of year would desecrate them, rendering them no longer kosher, or ceremonially clean and set apart for eating the ordained unleavened foods. This is a picture of consecration.

An essential furnishing of all Jewish houses of worship is its Ark, the special cabinet that holds the Torah scrolls, the Hebrew Holy Scriptures. At the synagogue I attended as a girl, the Ark resided behind a richly embroidered velvet curtain. Its white interior was illuminated, and whenever it was opened, the bright, white light spilled out into the sanctuary. I thought surely God Himself lived in there. It was the epitome of holiness, a place I never even dared to touch. That brightly lit little closet was created for just one purpose: to house those venerated parchment scrolls. It will never be used to store coats, shoes, sporting equipment, or even someone's best china. It is consecrated, sanctified, set apart for a holy purpose.

Alan and I have attended mass on various occasions. We've seen a priest, clothed in ceremonial robes and using an aspergillum, sprinkle holy water on the congregants and distribute the elements of the Eucharist following a prescribed order of service. Despite our lack of Catholic upbringing, we would never consider giving an aspergillum to a toddler to use as a teething ring. Nor would we give children communion wafers and wine as though they were snack-time juice and crackers at a daycare center. These items, too, are consecrated.

The word "consecrate" means to set something apart as holy. President Abraham Lincoln used the word in his Gettysburg Address when he said that the Civil War cemetery grounds had been consecrated by the thousands of Union soldiers who had risked and lost their lives there. Since November 19, 1863, that land has been set aside to memorialize and honor those men. In 1895, it was included with portions of the battlefield to form Gettysburg National Military Park. No one will ever construct a highway, shopping center or condominiums on that land.

The Bible abounds with references to holiness and consecration. God's Word makes it clear that things dedicated to Him and His service must be completely given over to Him, totally released from the hand of the giver. Second Samuel 23 tells how three of King David's mightiest warriors risked their lives to bring him water from a well then under the control of his enemies the Philistines. When they presented the water to David, he refused to drink it, but poured it out to the Lord.

In contrast to this total release, a couple named Ananias and Sapphira obtained infamous status in the fifth chapter of the book of Acts by pretending that they were giving the entire proceeds from the sale of some land to the apostles, when in reality they kept some for themselves. Unified in their conspiracy, they individually bore the consequences of lying to God when He required their lives. Consecration is an all-or-nothing affair.

You cannot partially consecrate your marriage relationship. It's either entirely set apart to God or it's not. And if your marriage belongs to God, then—and this may come as a surprise—it doesn't belong to you. You and your spouse are set apart together to show the world how God loves His people. You are His living illustration of self-sacrificing love in action. You do not have the right to not love your mate. You do not have the right to be unfaithful. And if your marriage is consecrated, then it's also holy.

Our friend Dr. Frank Seekins has spent many years studying and defining the ancient Hebrew pictographic alphabet. Believing that each letter represents both a sound and a concept, he has created fascinating and insightful studies of what he calls "Hebrew word pictures." I'm particularly fond of languages and the etymology, or root meanings, of words, and after the nine years of Hebrew lessons I attended as a child, I'm often awed to learn the deep, underlying meanings of blessings I recited by rote.

So I asked Frank about the Hebrew word for "holy," q'dosh. I already knew that it's made up of three Hebrew letters: quf ק, dallit ד and sheen שׁ. But the ancient letters look different, and each has its own meaning:

Quf ? = the back of the head, or something that follows another thing.

Dallit ד = the door or passageway.

Sheen ש = teeth or devouring.

Moreover, the dallit and sheen together form a word that means "to thresh." Thus the picture of q'dosh is "that which follows threshing."

In ancient Israel, as in nonmechanized agrarian societies today, the individual grains of wheat needed to be collected from the wheat plant after harvesting. So farmers would take their crop to a place called the threshing floor where they would lay the wheat stalks on the ground and beat them with an instrument to separate the straw from the heads. What was left of the wheat would still have a fibrous outer shell called the chaff. The threshers would toss the wheat into the air, and the wind would carry away the chaff while the heavier kernels of wheat would fall to the ground. Threshing is a long, arduous process, but what is left afterwards is the most valuable, and only edible, part of the plant.

So the Hebrew word picture of "holy," or what follows threshing, is the valuable, useful thing that is left after all the useless stuff has been beaten out of it. In other words, holiness isn't easy. It doesn't come to us naturally. It requires a painful process of getting rid of what God doesn't want in us, so that we can be used for His purposes.

We're not talking here about sexual fidelity. We hope that by this point in the book you know that you and your spouse are meant to be exclusively monogamous. Consecrating your marriage begins with a commitment much deeper than merely "forsaking all others." Consecration is not about all the things you won't do, as though you're depriving yourself of the fun things in life. The picture of Adam and Eve in the Garden is not one of deprivation. We call their innocent state "paradise." Their lives were rich and purposeful, free of guilt and shame, and fully devoted to God.

We bemoan their fall and the tragedy of sin entering the world. We long for a return to their perfect world, but as our daughter-in-law, JJ, expresses in her song "Garden Variety," "We hum the melody, but can't recall the words."

Jesus is the gate that allows you and your spouse to re-enter paradise. Naked and unashamed, you can commune with the Lord in the cool of the day as Adam and Eve did. But also as they did, you must present yourself before Him daily. You must allow no lesser, though more demanding, gods to get between you and Him. You must decide, you must choose, and you must do the most simple, yet most difficult daily act of letting go of control of your own life and pouring it out as an act of consecration before the Lord.

And men, you priests of your home, you must cover your wife and family with your prayers for them. Do not take your position as their authority and covering lightly. God doesn't; neither does Satan. Protect them; you have the spiritual mandate from the Lord to accomplish it.

And women, support your husband in this role. Pray for him and for his guidance from the Lord. Put yourself willingly under his protective care, and don't undermine his efforts to lead you. Allow him to serve you communion, and receive from him the bread and wine of Christ's love for you.

And both of you, pour yourselves out daily, emptying yourselves of your selves and your own agendas for your life and marriage. Then together drink deeply of all His Holy Spirit offers you.

KEY-TURNING APPLICATION

1. If you have never consecrated your marriage to the Lord, discuss the possibility of doing so now. If you're not sure how to consecrate your marriage, remember that God is not as interested in the particular words you speak as in your heart. If the two of you go together before God, and in sincerity express to Him your desire to dedicate your marriage to Him for His purposes, God will certainly honor that request.

Consider renewing your marriage vows. If you would like to do this right now, use the vows we've included on the next page, or you may compose your own. You may exchange your renewal vows privately or in a celebration that you plan for a future date attended by family and friends.

MARRIAGE VOW RENEWAL

I, _____, now choose to renew my pledges to you, _____, before God and this company of witnesses. I receive you as the helpmate and companion whom God has chosen for me. Knowing that you are my comrade and friend, I choose to treat you as a joint heir with me of the grace of life. I will share with you my companionship throughout life. I commit myself to you afresh today, irreversibly closing all "back doors" in our relationship. I will work together with you to resolve conflict rather than running from it or avoiding it. I will take responsibility for my part and will confess and ask your forgiveness for any known sins against you. In all my communication with you, I will strive for honesty and sensitivity. I will listen to you and respect your views and feelings.

I choose you above all others, and now today I recommit myself to you as your partner, lover, and friend.

_____
Signature

Signed this _____ day of _____, 20____.

chapter eighteen

WELCOME BACK TO REAL LIFE

LADIES AND GENTLEMEN

Having drunk from the cup, you remain kneeling next to each other, breathing prayers of thanksgiving to God for His grace and for giving you each other to love. Outside the chapel, the soft night air also breathes with the chirping of crickets and a whispering hint of a breeze.

"Look at the stars," says your spouse, and you both lie on your backs, gazing up through the clear ceiling. Its crystalline composition magnifies and sharpens the heavenly spectacle, the vast array of galaxies and nebulae, and you feel yourself on the edge of grasping infinite truths and mysteries long hidden from man. You're dizzy with the sensation of being caught up by a force of immeasurable strength, yet you're not afraid as it lifts you and your spouse beyond the realm of conscious thought. You catch a glimpse of Mr. Michaels—at least you think it's he, but you don't know how you know that since he's about 8 feet tall with flowing silver hair and glowing golden-white robes glimmering in the starlight.

Now he's driving a chariot and two horses that appear to be made of fire—though not burning. He says nothing, yet you understand perfectly as he stretches out his hands to the two of you. You're weightless, carried—By thought? By will?—into that fiery chariot. You feel enveloped in love and peace and an inexpressible sense of joy. All is well. You close your eyes and breathe deeply of this moment, wanting it to last forever. You breathe . . . you breathe . . .

When you open your eyes, you're home, lying in your own bed, wrapped in the arms of your beloved. Did you really inherit a grand estate from a fabulously wealthy benefactor, or was it all a dream? Inhaling the familiar scent of the precious flesh on which your cheek rests, you decide it doesn't really matter whether or not you've got riches beyond your wildest dreams; you have this mate, this gift from God to you, and that's all that matters.

The sun is rising outside your bedroom window with the promise of a new day. Its light sparkles on something shiny attached to a purse on the dresser—a gold key.

THE END

appendix

HOW TO BEGIN YOUR WALK OF FAITH

Knowing Jesus Christ personally as your Lord and Savior is the most important key for your Marital Mystery Tour. If you've never accepted Him as the perfect sacrifice for your sins, or if you're not sure and would like to have that certainty, follow the steps below. We encourage you to read the verses we mention directly from a Bible so you can see them in their context:

1. Realize that God loves you with His infinite love and has initiated a plan to redeem you from your sin so you can spend eternity with Him.
    John 3:16 *For God so loved the world that He gave His only begotten Son that whoever believes in Him should not perish but have eternal life.*

2. Recognize that you were born into a state of separation from God (which equals spiritual death) by sin—both the original sin of the first man and your own self-centered attitudes stemming from self-will and pride. This separation creates an insurmountable gap between you and God, so that your

physical death someday will also result in the eternal continuation of the spiritual death in which all people naturally exist apart from God.

Romans 3:23 *All have sinned and fall short of the glory of God.*

Romans 6:23 *For the wages of sin is death.*

3. Know that God in His infinite love for you bridged this sin-gap and provided a substitute to die and pay the penalty for your sin through His perfect sacrifice, the Messiah, Jesus Christ, who is the only way to eternal life. God showed His approval of Jesus' sacrificial death by raising Him from the dead.

   Romans 5:8 *God demonstrates His love for us, in that while we were yet sinners, Christ died for us.*

   1 Corinthians 15:3-6 *Christ died for our sins . . . He was buried . . . He was raised on the third day according to the Scriptures . . . He appeared to Peter, then to the twelve. After that He appeared to more than five hundred . . .*

   John 14:6 *Jesus said to him, "I am the way, and the truth, and the life; no one comes to the Father, but through Me."*

   Acts 4:12 *And there is salvation in no one else; for there is no other name under heaven that has been given among men, by which we must be saved.*

4. You need to choose to accept the gift of Jesus' sacrifice on your behalf; this choice begins your walk with God into eternal life and gives you the power to live life the way God designed it to be lived.

   John 1:12 *As many as received Him, to them He gave the right to become children of God, even to those who believe in His name.*

   Ephesians 2:8-9 *By grace you have been saved through faith; it is the gift of God, not as a result of works, that no one should boast.*

Romans 10:9 *If you confess with your mouth Jesus as Lord, and believe in your heart that God raised Him from the dead, you shall be saved.*

What words should you say to receive Jesus? God is aware of what is happening in your heart, so your words may be simple and few (or you may ramble as Pauly did when she asked Jesus into her heart). You may pray something similar to this:

"Lord Jesus, I need You. Thank You for being the perfect sacrifice for the world's sins, for dying on the cross and making a way for me to have eternal life. I receive You into my life as my Savior and Lord. Thank You for hearing my prayer. Amen."

If you just prayed in faith and asked Jesus into your heart, then be assured that God heard your prayer and has sent His Holy Spirit to live within you and give you the power to continue living a life that is pleasing to Him. We encourage you to tell someone about your decision and to get involved in a local church where you can continue to learn about God's Word, the Bible. A Bible-centered church can also provide you with mentors to help you grow in wisdom and in your faith.

And please let us hear from you. We would be happy to send you materials to help you walk along Messiah's Way. You can find us on the Web at www.walkandtalk.org or write to us c/o Walk & Talk, P.O. Box 54103, Phoenix, AZ 85078-4103.

To order additional copies of

The Marital Mystery Tour

contact AMFM Press by

phone at
(480) 585-0109

or

on the Internet at
www.amfmpress.com

Printed in the United States
92272LV00004B/62/A